Alexander Raby, Ironmaster

Proceedings of a Conference held at
Cobham on 28 November 1998

edited by Glenys Crocker

Preface and Introduction	iii
The Raby Background: The Midlands, London and the Weald, *Jeremy Hodgkinson*	1
Iron Working in Northern Surrey, *John Potter*	9
Alexander Raby at Cobham, *David Taylor*	15
Downside Mill, Cobham, *Alan Crocker*	22
Raby's Mill at Addlestone, *David Barker*	29
Alexander Raby – Ironmaster and Coalmaster, *Lyn John*	35
Appendix: Summary of Raby entries in London trade directories, 1749–1811, *Peter Jenkins*	41
Index of Persons, Places and Organisations	42
Associated Organisations	44

Surrey Industrial History Group
2000

Published by the Surrey Industrial History Group, c/o Surrey Archaeological Society, Castle Arch, Guildford GU1 3SX
SIHG Website: http://shs.surreycc.gov.uk/sihg/

© SIHG and the authors
ISBN 0 9523918 9 9

Principal Contributors

David Barker is Chairman of the Addlestone Historical Society.

Alan Crocker is President of the Surrey Industrial History Group.

Jeremy Hodgkinson is Chairman of the Wealden Iron Research Group.

Lyn John works in the steel industry and is a member of the Friends of Llanelli Museum.

John Potter is a Visiting Professor in the European Institute of Health and Medical Sciences at the University of Surrey and in the Postgraduate Institute of Sedimentology at the University of Reading.

David Taylor is President of the Esher District Local History Society.

Visit to Downside Mill by delegates to the Conference. The photograph, looking towards the south, shows the wheelpit of Alexander Raby's iron mill. This is located towards the top of the section of the plan on the back cover, between the Forge and the Tilt. The derelict waterwheel is a replacement of one of those on the plan.

Printed by J W Arrowsmith Ltd, Bristol

1762

Cover: *Plan of Cobham [Downside] Mills belonging to Alexander Raby, c.1798, from the Buttriss Archive.*

Preface and Introduction

In 1964 George Buttriss, an economic historian at Brooklands College, Weybridge, started to collect information about Alexander Raby with a view to writing his biography. Unfortunately he was unable to complete this project and shortly before he died in 1990 asked his wife to transfer the material to David Barker, Alan Crocker and Jeremy Hodgkinson on the understanding that it be lodged in an appropriate library for reference purposes. As the Buttriss Archive, it has been deposited in the Research Collections of the Surrey Archaeological Society at Castle Arch, Guildford.

Together with John Potter and David Taylor, the three recipients held discussions about the possibility of completing Buttriss's biography but concluded that they were unable to undertake this task. However, the idea of holding a one-day conference was attractive and resulted in a meeting held at Cobham on 28 November 1998. The *Proceedings* of this meeting are published in this volume. In the meantime, research on Raby's activities at Llanelli had been undertaken by Lyn John and he was invited to give a paper on this subject.

A conscious decision was made not to extend the scope of the conference to include Raby's activities in Derbyshire which have already been discussed by S D Chapman in his book *Stanton and Staveley: a Business History* (Woodhead-Faulkner, 1981). Briefly, between 1792 and 1805 Raby and partners operated the Dale Abbey ironworks at Stanton, which had been established on the estates of Charles, third Earl Stanhope, in 1787.

In addition to the work carried out by George Buttriss, significant contributions to research on Raby in Surrey have been made by the late Conway Walker of Cobham and the late George Greenwood of Walton-on-Thames. Their work is referred to in notes to the published papers.

Thanks are due to Cobham Methodist Church for providing a venue for the Conference, to Dominic Combe for allowing delegates to visit Downside Mill and to Carrie Taylor for helping with arrangements.

The authors are indebted to Glenys Crocker for editing and designing this volume, which has been published with the support of the Surrey Archaeological Society.

Alan Crocker, Conference Chairman
Castle Arch, Guildford

Alexander Raby (1747–1835). Photograph of a missing portrait, reproduced by courtesy of Llanelli Public Library.

Editorial note and Acknowledgements

The papers as presented at the Conference were revised by the authors following discussion at the meeting. Some points raised in discussion are reported in end-notes and cross-references are given between papers where appropriate. The paper by Alan Crocker on Downside Mill was delivered as an introduction and guide to the site visit on the day of the Conference and has been significantly expanded in the published version.

The large number of illustrations shown at the Conference have, of necessity, been reduced to a select few in the volume.

Two delegates to the Conference made their research notes available for viewing. Notes by P J Benians, including lists of material in the Corporation of London Record Office and transcripts of Freedom Documents, have been deposited, together with other material relating to the Conference, with the Buttriss Archive. A summary of Peter Jenkins' list of entries in London Directories is printed at the end of this volume. Other displays were as follows:

> John Potter: Specimens of slag. These are described in an Appendix to his paper.
> Surrey Industrial History Group: Downside Mill, Cobham.

Wealden Iron Research Group: Reconstruction drawings of iron-working by Reg Houghton.

Thanks are due to Clive Davies and Llanelli Public Library for image processing of the Raby portrait and the Surrey History Service for help with illustrations.

The Raby Background: The Midlands, London and the Weald

JEREMY S HODGKINSON

Members of the Raby family were living in the parish of Old Swinford in Worcestershire as far back as the sixteenth century, when an Edward Raby made his will in 1544. However, it has not been possible to trace a clear descent to the family who moved to London at the beginning of the eighteenth century. The first positive evidence of the Raby family's background in the iron trade is William Raby, a smith, of Old Swinford, whose son, Edward, was apprenticed to Ambrose Crowley in 1693.[1] Crowley, who was later knighted, was to become a major producer and distributor of ironwork, and the most prominent importer of Swedish iron into England. His father, also Ambrose, was based in Stourbridge, which lay in Old Swinford parish, where he had started as a nail maker.[2] In time he came to operate several forges in the area, putting out the bar iron he produced to local slitters and nailers. He also made steel, using Swedish iron in preference to the lower-quality, local metal. By the 1680s he had a 'steel house' at Stourbridge, from where he sold steel to customers over a wide area of the west Midlands, mostly in small quantities but also as hammers and anvils. Ambrose Crowley also had interests in South Wales where, in partnership with Major John Hanbury, he operated furnaces near Cardiff and Swansea, making iron for the production of tin plate.[3]

His son left Stourbridge in 1685, moving to Sunderland, where he set up a nail-making factory; five years later moving his works to Winlaton, six miles from Newcastle. From here he moved down into the valley of the Derwent to Winlaton Mill, where he built two steel furnaces and later expanded his business along the valley to Swalwell, where he built a further two steel furnaces.[4] It was while he was at Winlaton that Ambrose Crowley agreed to take as apprentice Edward Raby. Crowley was a member of the Worshipful Company of Drapers in the City of London, and had begun to take apprentices in 1684, before he had left Stourbridge.[5] The family's increasing wealth, and the importance of their business country-wide, had caused them to base themselves near London, at Greenwich, where Ambrose Crowley sought both social and business influence. Belonging to the Drapers' Company was not inconsistent with his trade in iron for, then as now, membership of a city livery company conferred status rather than indicating a particular business interest. It is significant that most of Ambrose Crowley's apprentices did not become freemen of the City of London, a reliable route to commercial influence. Instead, coming from provincial origins, as many of them did, they would have probably returned to their roots. Such may have been the case with Edward Raby. We do not know where he served his apprenticeship; whether he remained at the family's works around his native Stourbridge area, or gained experience in the North East. At some stage he may have worked in London; later connections suggest this.

The term of Raby's apprenticeship ended in 1701, and it appears that he continued to work for Crowley, returning to Stourbridge where, in the following year Ambrose Crowley's clerks were pressing Sampson Lloyd, Crowley's brother-in-law and fellow ironmonger, to make regular payments of £150 or £200 to Mr Raby & Co. at Stourbridge.[6] This implies that Raby had his own business, but intermittent references to Raby over the next ten years suggest that Raby was acting as agent for Crowley, and that the latter relied on Raby to deal with business in the Stourbridge area for him. As late as 1729, in an inventory of the estate of Ambrose Crowley's son John, there is mention of £9 owing to Edward Raby.[7] Given the extent of the Crowley family's interests in the area, as well as its importance nationally, Raby's role as agent was a position of considerable responsibility. The town was playing an increasingly important part in the iron industry of the west Midlands, with not only the Crowleys being influential there. The 'Ironworks in Partnership', formed in 1692 by the Foley family and others, resulted in an integrated network of ironworks stretching from the Forest of Dean to Staffordshire. A major element in that partnership centred on the Stour valley, and indeed the Foley family's involvement in the iron trade had begun in Stourbridge in the first half of the seventeenth century with Richard Foley, whose interest in the nail trade led eventually to the ownership of several furnaces. The partnership drew upon the Forest of Dean for its supplies of cast iron, refining the iron in the Stour valley forges and blending it with poorer, local cast iron.[8] Ambrose

Crowley did business with the Foleys, buying rod iron from them and, on occasions, having bar iron slit at the partnership's mills.[9] In 1703 Crowley noted that Raby had been dealing with Richard Wheeler, one of the partners.[10] After 1705, the partnership was reorganised, with many of the Stour valley forges being taken over by Richard Knight, who had joined their number, and who formed his own Stour Partnership in the early 1720s.[11]

Edward Raby's position as agent for the Crowleys at Stourbridge would have placed him in the midst of this thriving industrial landscape, allowing him to gain a wide knowledge of the industry as well as giving him the opportunity of building up a useful group of contacts in the iron trade. Whether there is a direct family connection between this, first, Edward Raby and a second of that name is unclear, but there is some circumstantial evidence to suggest such a link. Some eight years after the first Edward Raby began his apprenticeship with Crowley, Alexander Master, the son of Walter Master, a merchant, was also bound to Ambrose Crowley, through the Drapers' Company, gaining his freedom in 1711, by which time he was established as an ironmonger at Smithfield in London.[12] On 26 June 1746 Alexander Master's daughter, Mary, married an Edward Raby at St James's Church, Clerkenwell; the *Gentleman's Magazine* noting that she brought £15,000 to the marriage.[13] According to the marriage licence, for which he had paid £200, Raby was 23 years old.[14] He obtained his freedom in the Wheelwrights' Company by redemption (i.e. purchase) later in the same year, the documents noting that he was the 'son of Edward Raby late of London ironmonger decd'.[15] From this it can be inferred that Raby had not served an apprenticeship with a City livery company. It should also be recalled that the earlier Edward Raby had not been made a freeman. It is likely that Raby was working for Alexander Master, for when Master died in 1744 Raby took over what was undoubtedly a very lucrative ironmongery business in partnership with his brother-in-law, also named Alexander, who had been apprenticed to his father and had gained his freedom by patrimony (i.e. because his father had become a freeman of the City before his son's birth). In the late 1740s Edward Raby and Alexander Master's names began appearing together at the Smithfield address in the London commercial directories. In 1750 Raby 'translated' from the Wheelwrights' to the Drapers' Company.[16]

Within a year of their marriage, Edward and Mary Raby started what was to be a large family. Their eldest child, Alexander, born in 1747, was followed by six brothers and five sisters, although only five of the children survived into adulthood. Between 1749 and 1750 the family moved from West Smithfield to the St Margaret's Hill area of Southwark.[17] From 1759 Raby and Master occupied a warehouse in the Borough at the Bear Garden in Maid Lane.[18]

The late 1740s and 50s saw a temporary return to peace after nine years of overseas war, and business on the domestic iron market would have taken an upturn. We get an idea of the business that Edward Raby and Alexander Master did in this period from the detail of a warrant issued to them by the Board of Ordnance in March 1758 and delivered four months later.[19] In it were listed the various gauges of bar iron, staff iron and rolled plate that the partnership supplied. All were products of the forging process. They also produced both German and blister steel, and it is likely that Raby's father had gained experience of steel making in Stourbridge, where the Crowleys had a steel mill. It is probable that the partnership acquired their iron from Sweden, which was the main source for ironmongers in London, and the firm of Robert Macky, who was an importer, figures in the partnership's business in the next decade. The contract with the Board of Ordnance was to presage an important development in the partnership's business in the late 1750s.

Sometime in about 1758 – we do not know the details, the lease not having survived – Raby and Master acquired the tenancy of the Warren furnace, near East Grinstead in Sussex. Since the sixteenth century, the Weald of Sussex and Kent had become the principal source of heavy guns for the government service, and more than a century after the region had ceased to be the main area for iron production in the country, it retained the bulk of the contracts issued by the Board of Ordnance. This was largely due to the region's nearness to London, which was the principal market for such products, and also the skill of the local work force, which other regions had found difficulty in equalling. From the second half of the seventeenth century, London merchants had leased gunfoundries in the Weald to take advantage of the highly profitable trade in supplying both the government and the mercantile market with guns.[20] This trade had, of course, increased during times of war, of which there had been many up to the second decade of the eighteenth century. It had also been able to profit from the development of trans-oceanic shipping which British commercial exploitation in the Americas, Africa and the East had encouraged.

The War of the Austrian Succession, which had lasted from 1739 to 1748, had encouraged a small number of London founders and merchants to enter the ordnance trade and revive several furnaces in the Weald. The Crowley family had, themselves, entered this business in the 1730s, leasing furnaces at Ashburnham and Darwell.[21] The Peace of Aix-la-Chapelle left many of the conflicts in the war unresolved, and the renewed declaration of war in early 1756 had been anticipated to the extent that only one firm of Wealden gunfounders – William and George Jukes – had given up their lease in the meantime. Indeed, such was the perceived uncertainty of the peace that when their lease of Robertsbridge furnace and forge had fallen vacant in 1754, it was taken up by a founder from the Midlands, John Churchill.[22] The Seven Years' War of 1756–63 was waged over more fronts than any war hitherto, and the government's demand for ordnance was unprecedented and sustained.

The Warren furnace (TQ 348 393) had been built in 1567 and had been in blast until the early part of the seventeenth century.[23] From a contemporary map (figure 1) we know that the furnace pond was still in water, but it is unlikely that much of the infrastructure had survived.[24] A considerable amount of building work and repair must have been necessary to bring the site into use as a gunfoundry, involving substantial capital outlay. Watercourses had to be cleared, access routes re-established, and sources of ore and charcoal negotiated. At the same time the lease of Woodcock Hammer (TQ 369 419), a couple of miles downstream (figure 2), was purchased, to refine the surplus iron from the furnace, and possibly provide an extra source for the London works.[25] Skilled and unskilled labour had to be sought and, in the former case, housed. A pair of cottages built close to the furnace almost certainly date from this period, and there is a record of a group of closes being leased a short distance away, presumably for a similar purpose.[26] From the outset it seems likely that Raby was in charge of the operation, with Master continuing to supervise the Smithfield works. With forged iron products their usual stock in trade, entry into the smelting branch of the iron industry is likely to have been a radical departure for the partnership. Although both had a solid background in ironmongery, it is very probable that skilled founders and moulders had to be lured away from

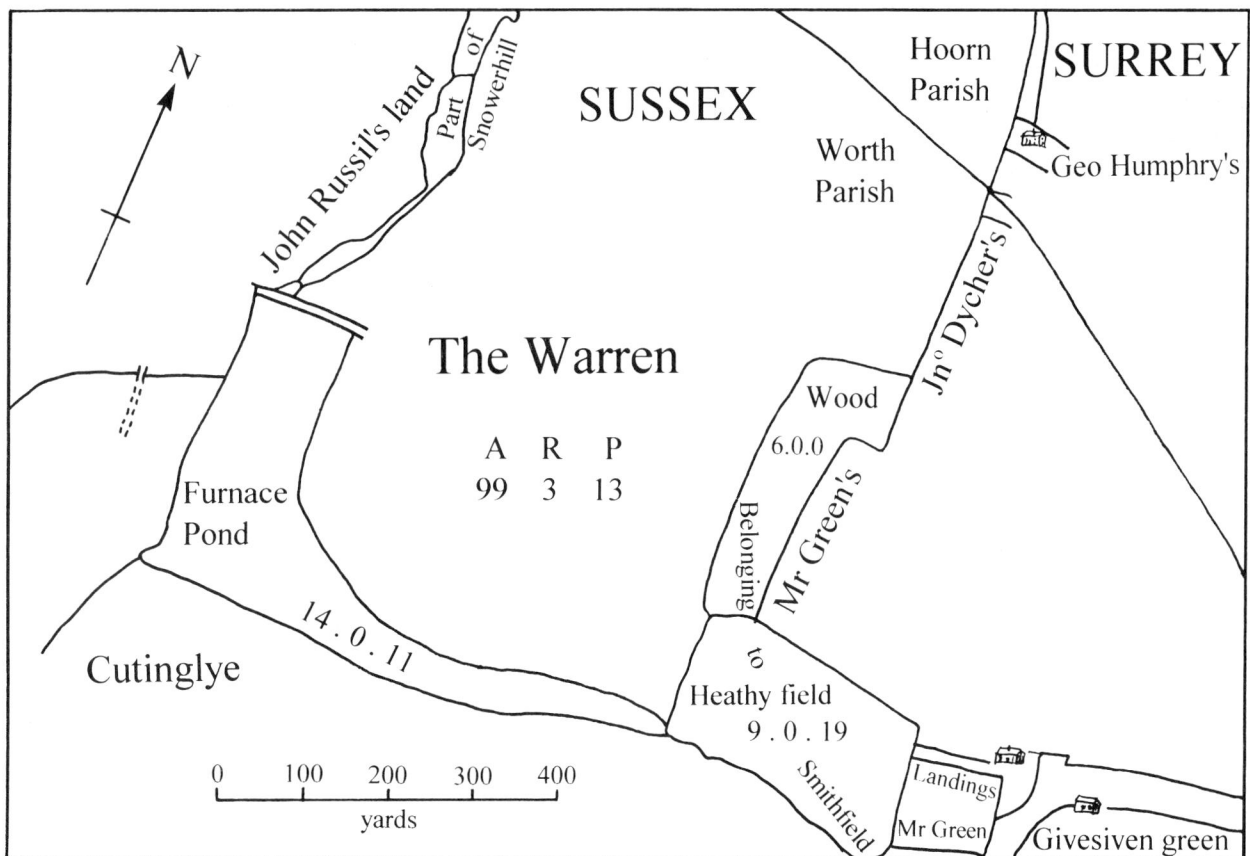

Figure 1. The site of Warren Furnace in 1748. Based on a map of the estate of Edward Evelyn held by the Mercers' Company, London. The modern spellings of Cutinglye, Givesiven and Hoorn are Cuttinglye, Gibbshaven and Horne. (Drawing by Alan Crocker)

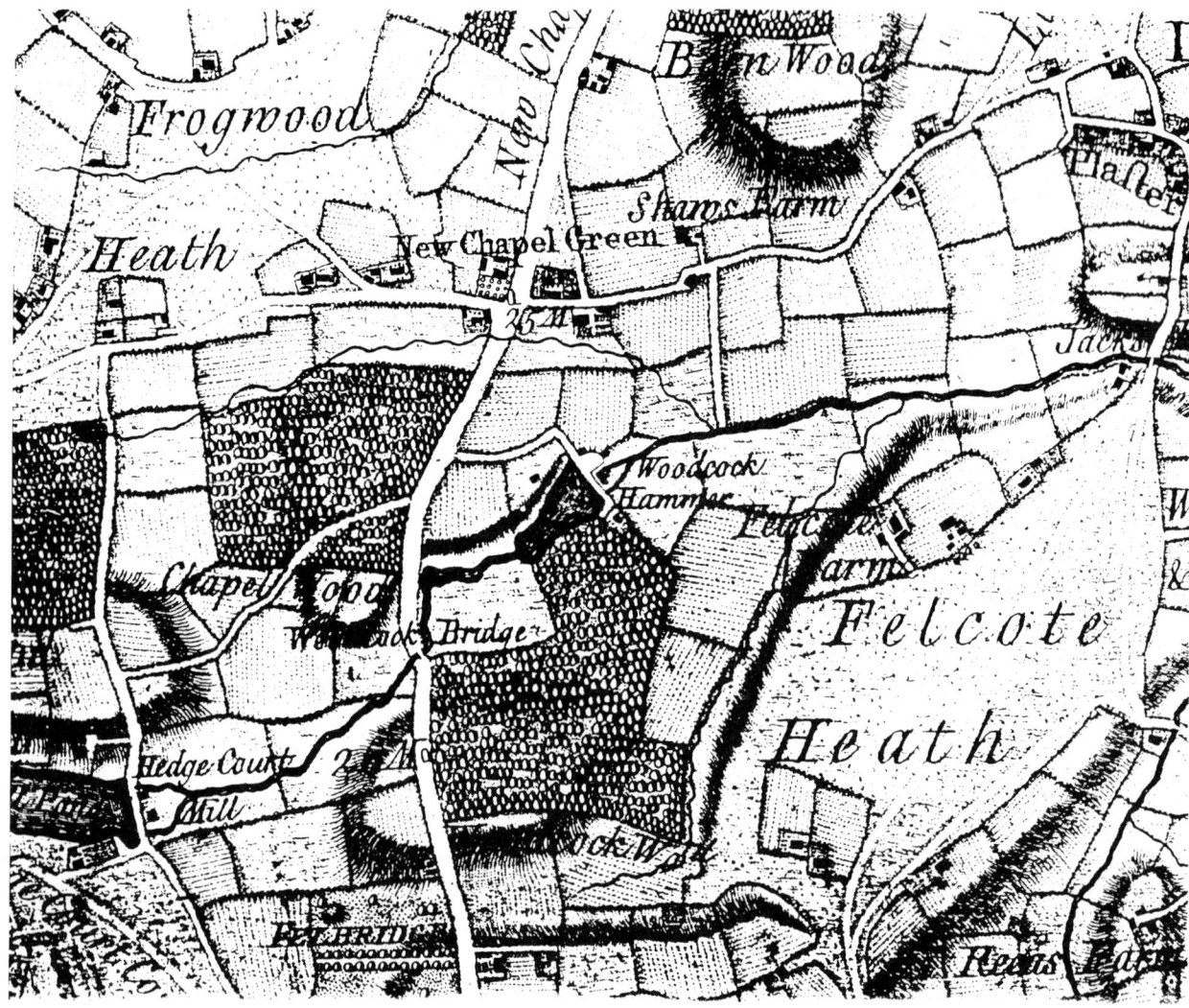

Figure 2. Woodcock Hammer, 1762 (J Rocque).

other furnaces, and it is likely that one of the reasons a furnace in the Weald was selected was the availability of skilled workers in the region.

In September 1758 Raby proposed to the Board of Ordnance that he cast 200 tons of iron ordnance and 200 tons of round shot, to be delivered during the following year at the prices paid to other founders.[27] With a few exceptions, Wealden furnaces produced, on average, about 250 tons of iron a year, so Raby must have set up an arrangement with another founder to produce about half of the order. This was later confirmed when he excused his failure to deliver some of the round shot on time by citing contrary winds and the lack of a convoy preventing the ships carrying the shot from Bristol.[28] The name of the supplier of the shot is not known, but it may have been Thomas Parker & Co. who had a foundry in Bristol at that time, and who were also casting guns for the merchant service.[29]

The war had been under way for three years when Raby's first delivery of guns arrived at the Royal Arsenal at Woolwich, and the issue of warrants to gunfounders had already passed its peak. The Board of Ordnance placed a further order with Raby in the early part of 1759, but in 1760 the Board, over-stocked after four years of re-equipping to fit out expeditions to North America and India, placed no orders for ordnance, almost certainly presenting the gunfounders, and not least Master and Raby who were only two years into this specialised branch of iron making, with acute problems of cash flow and debt repayment. This problem was offset by the partners securing orders for over £1700 worth of guns from the East India Company. Breaking into this market was to prove a lucrative sideline to their business with the government. The hiatus lasted a year, and warrants were issued again in February 1761, with Raby delivering nearly 400 tons to Woolwich that year, including a small consignment of guns cast with lifting rings, or 'dolphins' (figure 3). Raby was the only gunfounder who supplied these, and the skill required to cast them is an indication of the expertise which Raby's workmen possessed.

By 1762 France's sea power had been broken, and her armies in both India and North America had been defeated. However, perceiving a continuing threat from Spain, Britain declared war. The need for armaments continued and the government issued further warrants for guns and shot, Raby supplying over 400 tons, with the probability that again he sub-contracted the casting of shot. Although the majority of the information we have about Edward Raby's activities as a gunfounder comes from the records of the Board of Ordnance and the East India Company, from 1762 accounts of the transport of the products of the Warren furnace have survived. Robert Knight worked in the East Grinstead area carrying agricultural produce and timber to markets in south London.[30] He had also carried guns to Woolwich from Gravetye furnace, near West Hoathly, for William Clutton. On his journeys to Woolwich – a round trip of three days – as well as taking guns, he also brought back coal, probably for use in drying moulds. Occasionally Knight seems to have gone up to Smithfield as he records returning with steel, perhaps for use in the cutting edges for gun-boring bars. It is at this time that we first encounter Alexander Raby. In 1762 he had been apprenticed to his uncle, Alexander Master, at the age of fifteen, and was probably given experience at the partnerships' two sites, in London and in Sussex.[31] In 1764 Robert Knight recorded being paid 3 guineas by 'Allick' Raby, while the latter was assisting his father at the Warren furnace.[32]

The declaration of peace at the beginning of 1763 brought an end to the issue of all but a small number of warrants. The sudden cessation of hostilities and therefore of orders was a risk which affected all gunfounders, but particularly those, like Raby, who cast the larger guns. Only the Board of Ordnance placed orders for guns above 12 pounders, and the problem which faced the founders of 'great' guns, as John Fuller described them, was that there was no alternative market for such pieces if orders by the government were cancelled because of political expediency, or if such guns failed the rigorous government proof.[33] However, there was always a ready market in the mercantile sector for smaller guns, as most of the ships which plied the oceanic routes required a minimum armament for protection against pirates. Raby was able to continue to cast guns for the East India Company, and it is possible that he found a market amongst London merchants fitting out ships for overseas trade once the peace had made the trade routes more secure.

We do not know the circumstances which led, in November 1764, to Alexander Master and Edward Raby being declared bankrupt, but the fact that the principal creditor was named as Robert Macky, an importer of Swedish iron, suggests that it was in the ironmongery side of the partners' business that the

Figure 3. 12-pounder iron gun, with 'dolphins', cast by Master & Raby 1761–2; Woolwich Rotunda.

financial problems lay, and probably accounts for the disappearance of Alexander Master from among Raby's associates at this time.[34] That Raby was probably only bankrupted by virtue of his partnership with Master is suggested by the relative speed and confidence with which he set himself up again. In 1766, less than two years after being declared bankrupt, Raby wrote to the Board of Ordnance requesting orders, saying that his furnace in Sussex was in blast, and that he was prepared to accept the rate paid to other founders.[35] In the following February he was issued with warrants to supply the Board of Ordnance with 90 tons of guns.[36] The lease of both Warren furnace and Woodcock Hammer probably had several years to run, and in addition, Raby took the tenancies of Gravetye furnace and Howbourne forge. Gravetye, which had become vacant through another bankruptcy, that of William Clutton, lay about six miles south of the Warren.[37] It is likely that it had a relatively limited water supply, for Robert Knight recorded carrying guns from Gravetye to the Warren furnace, 'with their heads on', that is without having been bored.[38] Raby's occupancy of Howbourne forge, at Buxted, some 20 miles to the south east, was for just one year, and is, perhaps, only explicable in view of William Clutton's tenancy of the forge a few years earlier.[39] Raby cast guns at both of his furnaces, as well as shells at the Warren. Shells were another example of a specialised casting, and few founders made them. He also brought pig iron from London to Woodcock forge.

Raby's ability to retain orders from the Board of Ordnance in the period after the end of the Seven Years' War is all the more remarkable because the same period saw the dramatic intervention of the Carron Company, of Falkirk in Scotland. The price paid by the Board for guns reflected demand; rising at the beginning of the conflict when gunfounders could dictate the price for which they would supply ordnance, and falling again when peace was declared and the government's requirements enabled them to choose those founders who offered the lowest prices. In 1756 the Board had paid £15 a ton for the largest guns – 24 pounders and over – rising to £20 during the war.[40] Late in 1764, the Carron Company had offered to cast guns of all sizes for the Board, at £14 a ton, considerably undercutting all the other founders. In fact, only one founder, William Bowen, agreed to accept the same price; the others withdrawing from business with the Board. Carron had calculated on the coke-smelting process they were using being able to produce guns at a lower cost than the other founders, whose furnaces used charcoal. In fact the price Carron offered was £2 a ton cheaper than they could really afford, but their gamble was based on the hope that they would gain a monopoly, which they nearly did. The Board accepted Carron's offer and placed an order their way.[41] At this time Edward Raby was still extricating himself from bankruptcy. Nevertheless, he must have been confident of the viability of his business when he offered to cast for the Board again.

In the end, Raby did not do a great deal of business for the Board in the post-war years. The accounts of Robert Knight show that he carried a great many small calibre guns for Raby, none of which formed part of warrants issued by the government. At the same time, though, he was doing a profitable business with the East India Company, supplying guns, shot and shells for their forts and trading cantonments. From 1767 until 1771, Raby supplied the Company with over £14,000 worth of iron. It is also likely that he was continuing to cast guns for merchant shipping.[42]

In October 1770, Raby wrote to the Board of Ordnance saying that he had been casting brass guns for the East India Company, and offering to make similar castings for the government.[43] Technically bronze, but known as brass at that time, casting in this metal required a different process to iron smelting. The raw metal, often in the form of captured guns, was supplied by the Board of Ordnance and then melted in a reverberatory furnace. There was no necessity for water-powered bellows as in the case of a blast furnace, and this sort of hearth, which was also known as an air furnace, was most commonly found in urban foundries. By referring to his facility for turning, or finishing and boring the guns, by water, though, Raby implied that he was using one of his Sussex furnace sites for this work. Brass was in some ways easier to cast than iron, being a less volatile metal and, because of its structure, capable of producing more detailed castings. A skilled founder, as Raby clearly was, should have had no difficulties in transferring from one metal to the other. The Board accepted his offer and ordered sixteen mortars, to be made out of 50 tons of metal supplied to him.[44] An example is shown in figure 4.

In February 1771, Edward Raby died. We can only presume his death was sudden as he had made no will.[45] His widow took out letters of administration, but it would have been down to Alexander, as eldest son, aged 23, and less than a year after completing his apprenticeship, to take over his father's business.[46] In this he would have been

Figure 4. 8-inch land service brass mortar, Raby & Co., 1771 (cipher and inscription); Museo del Ejército, Madrid.

assisted by Mr Rogers, with whom Edward Raby had worked since being discharged from his bankruptcy, and who was probably the Obadiah Rogers who later worked with Alexander Raby in Surrey.

There were orders to meet for both iron and brass guns, and the furnaces would have been in blast at what was customarily the mid-point of the annual campaign. There were problems with the brass mortars ordered by the Board of Ordnance. Moulds needed to be made to take a fairly precise quantity of the metal, and from correspondence with the Board it is clear that Raby's workmen had been making the moulds too large. In July 1771 a letter had been sent to the Tower requesting a further 7 tons of brass to complete the order.[47] This prompted the Board to investigate the disparity in the weight of brass supplied and the number of guns cast. A comparison was ordered between Raby's mortars and those of another firm, Messrs English & Bradley, the result of which showed that the external dimensions of Raby's mortars were greater than they should have been, and that too much brass was being used.[48] The Board demanded payment for the excess metal which had been used, as well as arrears of proof fees for guns proved for the East India Company. Alexander Raby seems to have been reluctant to settle, and the dispute dragged on for three years. In March 1774 Alexander Raby wrote that he had 'left off the foundry business', although he continued to send iron mortars to Woolwich, hoping for the Warrants of Justification, that is to say warrants issued after delivery, which would secure payment.[49] In a last attempt to conclude his father's dealings with the Board of Ordnance Raby attempted to persuade the Board to forego the balance of £215 owing to them for brass metal he had used, but they stood firm. However, they agreed to settle at a higher price for some mortars supplied under an old warrant, stating, as they put it, that they did not 'choose to have a law suit'.[50]

In early 1773, Messrs. Wright & Prickett, gunfounders, who, four years earlier, had given up the lease of North Park furnace, near Haslemere, announced that they had taken two iron foundries in Sussex formerly occupied by Messrs. Master & Raby and Messrs. Harrison & Bagshaw.[51] There seems little doubt that the furnaces referred to were the Warren furnace, and the Gloucester furnace at Lamberhurst.

Alexander Raby's abandonment of gunfounding in 1774 was not the family's last association with the Weald, for he was to return in 1783 to take the tenancy of Abinger Hammer for four years, presumably in connection with his activities elsewhere in Surrey at the time.[52]

Notes and References

1. Surrey Archaeological Society Library: Research Collection, Buttriss Archive, Indentures of apprenticeship of Edward Raby 1693.
2. Flinn, M W, *Men of Iron*, (Edinburgh, Oliver & Boyd, 1962), 12.
3. Flinn, ref. 2, 13–15.
4. Barraclough, K C, *Steelmaking before Bessemer, Vol. 1: Blister Steel*, (London, Institute of Metals, 1984), 61–2.
5. Buttriss Archive, ref. 1, Percival Boyd to M W Flinn, 24 Nov 1952 (copy).

6. Friends' Meeting House, London, Lloyd Mss, Clerks of Ambrose Crowley (III) to Sampson Lloyd, Birmingham, 24 Oct 1702.
7. Suffolk Record Office: HAI/GD/4/13, Inventory of estate of John Crowley 1729.
8. Schafer, R G, 'Genesis and Structure of the Foley "Ironworks in Partnership" of 1692', *Business History*, **13** (1971), 19–38, at 33–5.
9. Flinn, ref. 2.
10. Ambrose Crowley (III) to Sampson Lloyd, 12 June 1703; H. Lloyd, private collection.
11. Ince, L, *The Knight Family and the British Iron Industry 1695–1902*, (London, Merton Priory Press, 1991), 1–3.
12. Corporation of London Record Office (CLRO): Alphabets of Freedom Admissions, CFI/288. I am greatly indebted to Mr Peter Benians for information about membership of City livery companies.
13. *Gentleman's Magazine*, 9 July 1746.
14. Guildhall Library, Calendar of Marriage Licences, 330/1746 June 25; Bond MS.10,091E/59 1746.
15. CLRO: Alphabets of Freedom Admissions, CFI/679.
16. Drapers' Hall, Minutes of the Court of Wardens, 10 June 1752.
17. Buttriss Archive, ref. 1, Raby family papers (copy).
18. Southwark Local History Library: Overseer's Rate Book, 1748–66.
19. Public Record Office (PRO): Board of Ordnance Bill Books, WO51/202, p.247.
20. Cleere, H F, & Crossley, D W, *The Iron Industry of the Weald*, (2nd edn, Cardiff, Merton Priory Press, 1995), 191–2.
21. Hodgkinson, J S, 'The Decline of the Ordnance Trade in the Weald; the Seven Years' War and its Aftermath', *Sussex Archaeological Collections*, **134** (1996), 155–67, at 156–7.
22. Whittick, C H C, 'Wealden Iron in California', *Wealden Iron* (Bulletin of the Wealden Iron Research Group), 2nd ser., **12** (1992), 29–62 at 56–62.
23. Cleere & Crossley, ref. 20, 364.
24. Mercers' Hall, Map of Estate of Edward Evelyn, 1748.
25. Cleere & Crossley, ref. 20, 366.
26. Surrey History Centre (SHC): K61/3/2.
27. PRO: Minutes of the Surveyor-General of the Ordnance: WO47/52, p.216.
28. PRO: WO47/54, p.507.
29. PRO: Registers of the Privy Council, PC2/106, p.210.
30. West Sussex Record Office: Add. Ms. 46,861.
31. Drapers' Hall: Apprenticeships, 13 May 1762.
32. Hodgkinson, J S, 1978, 'The Carrier's Accounts of Robert Knight, Part 2: The Accounts', *Wealden Iron*, **14** (1978), 11–24 at 15.
33. Crossley, D W, & Saville, R V, *The Fuller Letters: Guns, Slaves and Finance 1728–1755*, (Lewes: Sussex Record Society, **76**, 1991), 254–5.
34. PRO: B4/17 p.166.
35. PRO: WO47/68 p.133.
36. PRO: WO47/69 p.59.
37. Hodgkinson, J S, 1989, 'William Clutton – Ironmaster', *Wealden Iron*, 2nd ser., **9** (1989), 27–33.
38. Hodgkinson, ref. 32, 22–3.
39. East Sussex Record Office: ELT Buxted.
40. Hodgkinson, ref. 21, 166 n.29.
41. Hodgkinson, ref. 21, 161.
42. British Library Oriental & India Office Collection: L/AG/1/5/18–19.
43. PRO: WO47/76 p.187.
44. PRO: WO47/76 p.192.
45. Registers of St. Saviour's Church, Southwark; Raby was buried on 13 February 1771.
46. PRO: PROB6/147.
47. PRO: WO47/78 p.36.
48. PRO: WO47/78 pp.249 & 288.
49. PRO: WO47/83 p.163.
50. PRO: WO47/85 p.284.
51. PRO: WO47/81 f.99.
52. SHC: P1/6/1.

Iron Working in Northern Surrey

JOHN F POTTER

A full appreciation of the history of metal working at mill sites in northern Surrey is undoubtedly confused by the suggestion of early authors that the raw material – principally iron – was extracted locally.[1] This picture, and its unravelling, afford a record of coincidences. The final coincidence perhaps being that I was to become acquainted with Mr G E Buttriss without being aware, until his final years, that he had a particular interest in Downside Mill, and more especially in that mill's one time leaseholder, Alexander Raby.

Iron Age interventions

In 1911, Dr Gardner[2] described the presence of 'parallel trenches' which 'may be iron workings' on the northern slopes of St George's Hill, Weybridge. In 1915, he suggested[3] that these trenches might have been made in 'prehistoric times'. Coincidentally, the discovery of tokens (dated 1812, and illustrating the Weybridge iron mills as shown in figure 1) and a lease for an iron mill (dated 1779) was sufficient for Gardner, supported by the Geological Survey representatives, Dewey and Bromhead,[4] to conclude that the trenches instead, were of a much later period. The case was then set for others to claim that the ore for the mills was extracted from 'shallow trenches in and near St George's Hill, Weybridge'[5] and 'between 1779 and 1812'.[6]

My interests in historical metal working in northern Surrey originated from geological observations in the lower reaches of the Wey and Mole valleys, and in particular, to a geological section opened in the winter months of 1974–1975, for the then new dual-carriage construction on the A3 London to Portsmouth road, near its junction with Redhill Road (TQ 084 598). The temporary exposure revealed pyritous clays of the Lower Bracklesham Beds[7] and, more especially, two sideritic (iron carbonate) clay ironstone bands.[8] Coincidentally, the present author was invited to comment on the Iron Age excavations and the iron smelting furnaces discovered at the Brooklands site, Weybridge (TQ 068 632).[9] The siderite rich bands provided an adequate source of high quality iron for such small scale, relatively low-temperature furnaces. The enclosing clays were also utilised to create a visibly distinctive pottery on the site.[10]

The Iron Age smelting furnace studies at the Brooklands site and elsewhere in northern Surrey,[11] convinced me that the trenches at the lower levels of the outcrop of the Bracklesham Beds at St George's Hill, Weybridge, had been created in Iron Age times. The occurrence of these trenches is shown in figure 2. The conclusion automatically followed that the northern Surrey iron mills were essentially used for forging, i.e. for the conversion of cast iron into wrought iron products. This was based on the following principal arguments:

(a) Most Wealden iron furnace (i.e. smelting) activity terminated in the eighteenth century.[12] It was unlikely that a Weybridge-area iron industry would have developed and been economically viable in a period when the much bigger Wealden Industry was in decline.
(b) The method of exploitation of the Weybridge ore,[13] in trenches, some 'spread out in a sheaf' was dissimilar to the bell-pit or minepit technique used throughout the Weald in more recent times.[14]
(c) There was evidence that iron was brought up the Thames to be worked, as for instance in 1802,[15] and that the mills marketed their iron products, such as barrel hoops, plate, nails and wire, at downstream destinations.[16]
(d) Several of the iron-working mills had previously operated as copper or brass forging mills. The

Figure 1. Rubbing of token issued in 1812 by John Bunn & Co., illustrating the Weybridge Iron Mill.

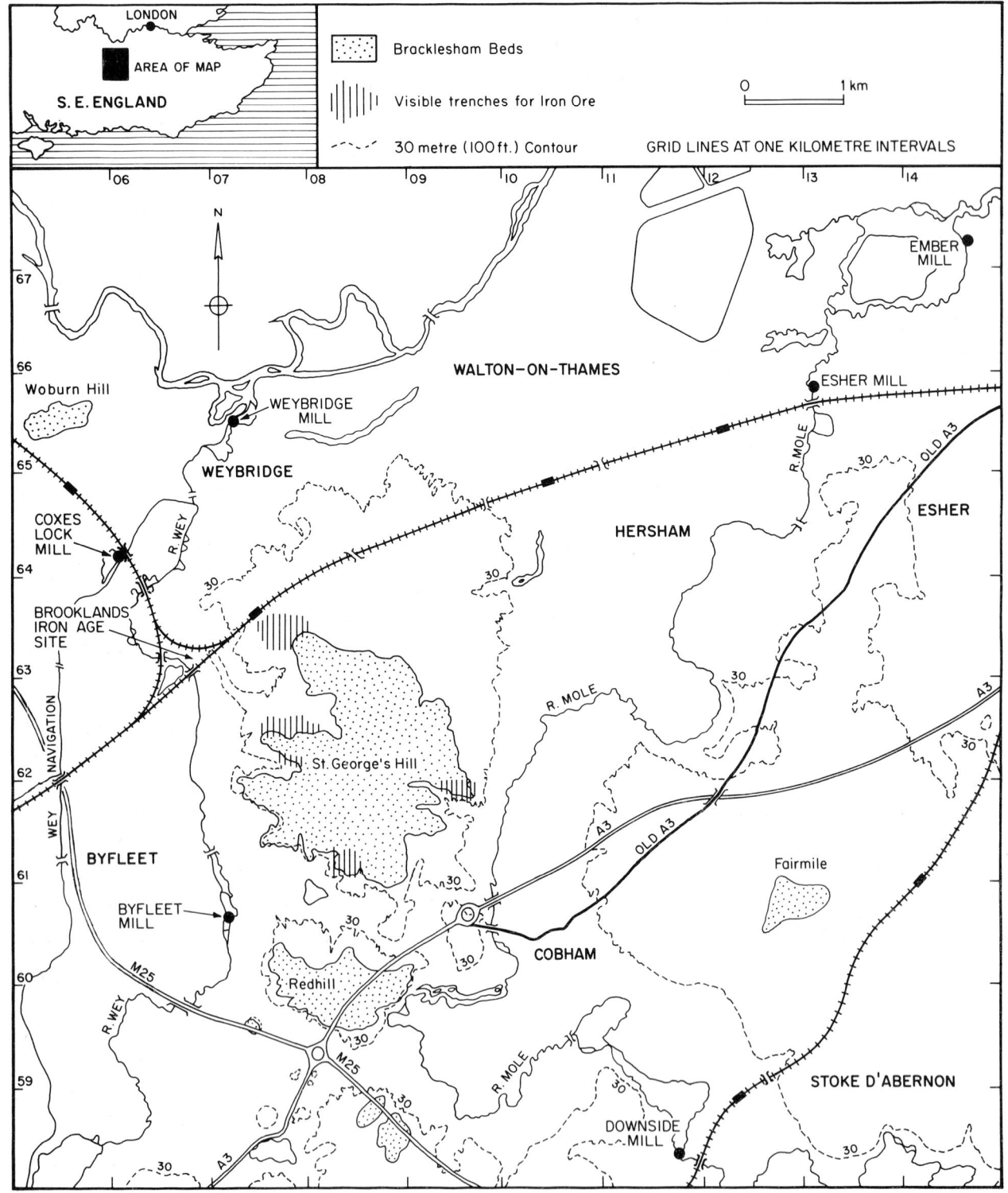

raw material for these processes had clearly been imported into the region. There was a precedent for the importation of the raw material.

(e) Each iron working mill discovered was situated on a principal river (the Wey or Mole) or on the Wey Navigation. Straker[17] recognised that mills sited on larger rivers, where a relatively constant flow of water was available, were typically more continuously-operating forges rather than furnaces.

(f) There was a total absence of any contemporary records of extraction of ore in the area during the seventeenth, eighteenth and nineteenth centuries.

Further reasons for historic iron-forging practices have been cited elsewhere.[18]

The Iron Mills

The investigation for iron mill forging sites in the region was undertaken in 1977 by searching the banks and beds of the water courses for evidence of iron slags. These slags represented the waste element of the forging processes and were frequently dumped in the proximity of the mill. Prior to the 1977 study, three mills – the Weybridge mill recorded on the preserved token, Coxes Lock mill in Addlestone and Downside mill – were the only ones in the region thought to have been involved in iron working. Six major mill sites particularly involved in iron fabrication were discovered in the region (figure 2 and table 1) and, in three of these, the literature records show that Alexander Raby had an interest.

For successful operation, the water requirements of an iron mill are more demanding than for those of other milling processes. A large head or volume of water is required to work iron compared with softer, more malleable metals like copper, brass and lead. In about 1783, for instance, Raby constructed a large reservoir at Coxes Lock Mill in Addlestone to provide a continuous and more powerful water supply for his forge. The lower reaches of the Wey and more especially the Mole,[19] have unusually steep profiles in the vicinity of the river-based mills (Byfleet, Downside and Esher mills), and this was presumably one reason for the iron-working activities in the area. Northern Surrey obviously had certain other attractions to the industrialists of the period. Many of the mill owners had additional properties and marketing outlets in central London. The proximity of the London market must have been commercially important, particularly as the mills were far enough away from London to avoid the restrictions imposed by the City Livery Companies.

Neither the Wey nor the Mole is easily navigable. The more remote Raby mill at Downside, Cobham, for instance, was particularly reliant on horses for the conveyance of iron for fabrication from, and manufactured articles to, the River Thames or the Wey Navigation at Weybridge. The abundance of stabling on the Downside site can still be noted and an old sketch once existed[20] of horses transporting iron ware through Weybridge for subsequent carriage to London by barge.

In 1763 the navigation of the River Wey was extended to Godalming and from that date, it was possible that some iron for the mills was obtained via the canal from Wealden smelting furnaces. Possibly the nearest furnace was then at Thursley to the south-west of Godalming.[21]

The mills of Alexander Raby

Downside Mills, Cobham, River Mole (TQ 117 583)

A mill is known to have existed on this site from as early as 1331 and in the eighteenth century it operated both as a corn and a paper mill prior to becoming an iron mill.[22] Alexander Raby, born in 1747, was the son of Edward, a Southwark, London ironmonger.[23] He acquired the lease on Downe Mills (Downside) in 1770 in conjunction with a Mr Mereton. At first Raby lived in the house adjoining the mill and converted the mill for iron fabrication.

Table 1. Summary of iron-working activities of mills

Mill	Location	Suggested dates	Activities
Byfleet	R. Wey TQ 073 607	1675–1703	Limited iron manufacturing (with paper)
		1703–1754	Limited iron manufacturing (with copper and brass)
		1754–1806	Iron
Weybridge	R. Wey–Wey Navigation TQ 073 655	1720–1764	Iron manufacturing (with corn and brass)
		1764–1817	Iron
Coxes Lock*	Wey Navigation TQ 061 642	1777–1807	Iron and possibly corn†
		1807–1831	Iron
Downside*	R. Mole TQ 117 583	1771–1798	Iron
		1798–1807	Iron and copper
Esher	R. Mole TQ 133 658	1785–1815	Possibly a little iron, mainly corn
Ember*	R. Ember TQ 146 673	1693(4)–1802	Iron, with brass and corn

*Mills in which Alexander Raby obtained an interest.
†See note 35.

Locally, the Byfleet, Weybridge and Ember mills were already established as iron manufacturing sites (table 1) and a precedent existed in the area for this type of operation. By 1781, the site included, in addition to the messuage, two workshops, a stable, the iron mill, two forges and more than 9 acres (3.6 ha) of land, at a rent of £40 per annum.

The workings and buildings on the site were gradually extended by Raby until in about 1798 (cover illustration) the site also included a copper mill. The importance of stabling to the business has already been noted. Raby is known to have had a partnership in a shop at 31 Greek Street, Soho, where his manufactured articles were sold.[24] He probably developed still further outlets for his iron ware in these latter years of the eighteenth century, for about this time he held additional interests in both the Coxes Lock and Ember Mills. He had the use of premises at 9 All Hallows Lane, Upper Thames Street, London (Steelyard), over the period 1785–1805.[25] Raby also acquired property interests elsewhere in London, for instance, in Bush Lane,[26] (near Cannon Street Station) and locally the lease on a Josiah Wedgwood property at Stoke House, Stoke D'Abernon.[27] The success of Raby's many entrepreneural activities during the 1790s have been highlighted by Buttriss[28] and others.[29]

A map dated 1807[30] shows the iron mill still in Raby's possession, but by then he had moved from the district to assist in pioneering the South Wales iron industries. He died in Somerset in 1835.

After Raby's departure, Downside mill was converted to a flock mill for processing rags. A number of his original buildings are still present on the site although the copper mill is only represented by its sluice. An unusual cottage on the site preserves a drying flue from the period of flock production.

Iron forge slag is abundant on the site and pieces of possible tap-slag have been found. The tap-slags are likely to be a by-product of casting processes from impure iron bars. The use of slag as a building material on the site is illustrated in figure 3.

More detailed accounts of Downside mill are given by Taylor and Crocker in papers 3 and 4.

Coxes Lock Mill, Wey Navigation Canal (TQ 061 642)

Coxes Lock[31] mill is believed to have been built in the period 1776–7, for operations commenced somewhat illegally in April 1777 when the canal bank was cut without permission to provide water to turn the wheel.[32] The mill seems to have been first operated by Alexander Raby in partnership with Obadiah Wix Rogers, described as an 'iron

Figure 3. Iron slag used to retain the bank of a water channel at Downside Mill, Cobham. The tunnel follows approximately the line of the legend 'Road to Down Farm' on the front cover map. Its outflow, towards the camera, joined the tail water of the copper mill which was to the left.

master of Thomas Street, Horsley Down'[33] (a street once just to the south-east side of Tower Bridge, London). By July 1782, they had secured an agreement[34] at a rent of £130 per annum, to cut channels into the canal to obtain water to drive their mill wheels. In 1783, permission was obtained by Raby to build a corn mill and to construct a hammer.[35] At about that time he acquired more land and constructed a large reservoir in order to maintain his water supply. The hammer which was built 'to beat down the ruff edges left on the iron by the cutters' was capable of striking 2700 blows an hour.[36] It acquired a reputation for noise and the name 'Hackering Jack'. The noise was such that objections were raised by Lord Portmore, one of the canal's proprietors and a resident of Weybridge. A minor feud developed, which continued for the major duration of Raby's leasehold.

In 1807, Raby and Rogers relinquished their licence to use the canal waters to John Taylor, iron merchant of All Hallows (beside Cannon Street Station), London. Following a number of different operators, iron fabrication ceased at the mill in about 1831. A plan of 1834[37] shows the former Raby foundry as waste land and the associated text indicates that its site was 'formerly overgrown with broom'. A new mill was rebuilt in about 1900 and the whole complex has now been extensively modified to provide residential housing. Although significant buried deposits exist it is now difficult to find iron forge slag on the site.

A more detailed account of Coxes Lock mill is given by Barker in this volume, pages 29–34.

Ember Mill, River Ember (TQ 146 673)

The River Ember is a short bifurcation of the Mole prior to its entry into the Thames. The earliest reference to a mill on the site is dated 1607. Brass wire production commenced at the mill in 1638, and from 1649 to 1663 or as late as 1670[38] the operation was managed by Jacob Momma and partners. The fabrication of iron products first commenced in 1693 or 1694, when John Stapleton and Christopher Trummer obtained a lease and erected a new mill on the site.

Over the next century the operation of the mill changed hands a number of times,[39] but in 1795, the lease passed to Alexander Raby. He manufactured iron ware at the site until 1802. The mill subsequently reverted to corn milling and was demolished in 1837. The mill sluices and a limited amount of iron slag are visible in the vicinity.

Other Sites

In addition to the mills that existed at Byfleet (TQ 073 607), Weybridge (TQ 073 655) and Esher (TQ 133 658), which have been described elsewhere,[40] two occurrences of deposited iron forge slag were discovered at TQ 107 595 and TQ 103 627. In the absence of documentary evidence for further mill sites, both these occurrences are thought to represent a depository site for waste from the Downside Mill. At the former site, on the river side of Cobham Park at Downside Bridge. the iron slag may well have been used to create a rubble wall for the dam of the ornamental lake in Cobham Park. It has been claimed incorrectly that the Cobham Park house provided a Raby residence at least over the period 1793 to 1795.[41]

Appendix: Exhibit of Iron Slags from northern Surrey

A number of typical iron slags from the vicinity of Downside Mill, Cobham and Coxes Lock Mill, Addlestone were exhibited. Most of these could be interpreted as slags resulting from the forging processes although a possible tap-slag from Downside was also on display. This type of tap-slag is considered to have been a by-product of casting processes from impure iron bars.

By contrast an iron slag from a bloomery at the Brooklands, Weybridge, Iron Age site was exhibited. The raw material utilised by the Iron Age workers, from iron carbonate (siderite) lenses and seams obtained in the area of St George's Hill and extracted a few metres from the base of the Eocene, Bracklesham Beds, was also displayed.

The author's work had also shown that the clay enclosing the iron carbonate seams had been used for Iron Age pottery, pieces of which were on display. These could be compared with a sample of the clay which had been recently fired.

Notes and References

1. Dewey, H & Bromehead, C E N, *The Geology of the Country around Windsor and Chertsey* (Memoir of the Geological Survey of England and Wales, 1915); Gardner, E, 'Weybridge and Byfleet: Traces of old Iron Works', *Surrey Archaeological Collections (SyAC)*, **34** (1921), 115–116; Hillier, J, *Old Surrey Water-mills* (Skeffington, 1951); Lansdell, A, *The Wey Navigation* (Elmbridge Borough Council, 1975); Sherlock, R L, *British Regional Geology London and Thames Valley* (HMSO, 1954).; Walker, T E C, 'Cobham: manorial survey', *SyAC*, **58** (1961), 47–78, at 47–8.
2. Gardner, E, 'The British stronghold of St George's Hill, Weybridge', *SyAC*, **24** (1911), 40–55.
3. Gardner, E, 'A Late-Keltic knife found at Weybridge', *SyAC*, **28** (1915), 183–4.
4. Dewey & Bromehead, ref. 1, 92.
5. See for example Hillier, ref. 1, 125.
6. See for example Sherlock, ref. 1, 64.
7. Potter, J F, 'Eocene, lower Bracklesham Beds iron workings in Surrey', *Proc Geologists' Association*, **88** (1977), 229–41.
8. Potter, J F, 'A Bracklesham-Bagshot Beds unconformity in the London Basin', *Proc Geologists' Association*, **97** (1986), 87–90.
9. Hanworth, R, 'Brooklands, Weybridge, TQ 068 623', *SyAS Bull*, **70** (1970); Hanworth, R & Tomalin, D, *Brooklands, Weybridge: the excavation of an Iron Age and Medieval site 1964–65 and 1970–71*, SyAS Research Volume, **4** (1977).
10. Potter, J F, in Hanworth & Tomalin ref. 9, 23; Potter, J F, 'Iron working in the vicinity of Weybridge, Surrey', *Industrial Archaeology Review*, **6** (1982), 211–23.
11. *Ibid*, 213–14.
12. Straker, E, *Wealden Iron* (Bell, 1931).
13. Dewey & Bromehead, ref. 1, 92.
14. Topley, W, The geology of the Weald. (Memoir of the Geological Survey, UK, 1875), 334; Straker, ref. 12; Worssam, B C, Iron ore workings in the Weald Clay of the Western Weald', *Proc Geologists' Association*, **75** (1964), 529–46.
15. Surrey History Centre (SHC): G129/35/6, G129/35/9.
16. Nash, M, 'Barge traffic on the Wey Navigation in the second half of the seventeenth century', *J Transport History*, 1970, 218–224.
17. Straker, ref. 12, 73.
18. Potter 1982, ref. 10, 213.
19. Bull, A J, Gossling, F, Green, J F N, Hayward, H A, Turner, E A & Wooldridge, S E, 'The River Mole: its physiography and superficial deposits', *Proc Geologists' Association*, **45** (1934), 35–69.

20. Weybridge Museum staff, pers. comm. (1980).
21. Straker, ref. 12, 191; Hadfield, C, *The Canals of south and south-east England* (David & Charles, 1979), 119; Vine, P A L, *London's lost route to the sea* (David and Charles, 1973), 18.
22. Walker, ref. 1, 1961.
23. Buttriss, G E, *Alexander Raby – a Surrey Iron Master* (Walton and Weybridge Local History Society Monograph, **34**, 1985) and pers. comm.
24. Univ. Keele Library Document 25491-128, dated 1800.
25. See summary of entries in London trade directories, page 41.
26. Univ. Keele Library Document 13307-77, 26 April 1794.
27. Univ. Keele Library Document 13310-77, dated 1799.
28. Buttriss, ref. 23.
29. For example, Innes, J, *Old Llanelly* (Western Mail Ltd, 1902), 104–6.
30. SHC: 2610/38/21: map of Cobham Manor. Taylor (this volume, ref. 25) comments that although this map is dated 1807, the information it provides on Downside Mills appears to be from the 1790s.
31. The modern spelling Coxes is used in the present volume. Alternative spellings are discussed by Barker, this volume, ref. 1.
32. SHC: G129/39/8.
33. SHC: G129/104/1.
34. SHC: G129/10/41.
35. SHC: G129/21/69. David Barker comments that, although Raby expressed his intention to erect a corn mill at Coxes Lock, there is no evidence that he did so, or that active corn milling took place there before 1834–5.
36. SHC: G129/42/2, reproduced in facsimile in Barker, this volume, page 32.
37. SHC: G6/2/68.
38. SHC: K61/5/15.
39. Potter 1982, ref. 10, 220.
40. Potter, ref. 7; Potter, ref. 8.
41. This claim, made by Innes, ref. 29, and reported by Buttriss, ref. 23, is discussed by Taylor, this volume, page 15. See also Crocker, this volume, page 26.

Alexander Raby at Cobham

DAVID TAYLOR

In February 1771 Alexander Raby's father, Edward, died suddenly and without making a will. Edward Raby had been in partnership with Alexander Master at one of the last of the Sussex iron works, the Warren Furnace at Felbridge. In the same year as his father's death Alexander married Ann Cox, daughter of the manager of the London showrooms of Josiah Wedgwood, who was a witness to the marriage settlement.

George Buttriss observed that 'even at the early age of 24 Raby was ready to embark on what was to be a very distinguished career. He was already a London iron merchant, a freeman of the City of London, a member of a City Livery Company and manager of the Warren Furnace which was producing iron goods (including ordnance) and was highly profitable'. He also suggested that Alexander was motivated to set up independently by the circumstances of his father's intestacy, which resulted in his mother Mary taking control of the family business.[1] However, Alexander had already acquired Down Mill at Cobham by the time of his father's death. The sale of the mill had come about through the bankruptcy of Joseph Hunt, paper maker, dealer and chapman, and the auction took place on 15 May 1770 at the White Lion in Cobham.[2] The property was described as:

> TO be Sold by AUCTION, by Mr. Salkeld, by order of the assignees, at the White Lion in Cobham, on Tuesday the 15th of May, at Twelve o'Clock, A PAPER-MILL, with House, Garden, &c. and a Freehold Messuage, the Lease (of which there were seventeen years and a half unexpired at Lady-day last) of that substantial Paper-Mill called DOWN MILL; situate in the Parish of Cobham, in the County of Surry, late in the occupation of Joseph Hunt, a bankrupt; together with the Dwelling-House, Out-Houses, Garden, and Orchard, with about an Acre of Land, and Half an Acre of Ozier Ground, subject, for the next Four Years to come, from Lady-day last, to the Rent of 35l. per Annum, for the remaining Thirteen Years and a Half of the Lease at 40l. per Annum.

Raby moved quickly to develop this site and between September 1770 and May 1771, he purchased over 52,000 bricks from The Hon. Charles Hamilton who had kilns in his park at nearby Painshill. The purchase of 12,000 plain tiles and 100 ridge tiles in November and December 1770 appears to indicate that the building was nearing completion at that time. In addition to bricks and tiles Raby also purchased from Hamilton several 'shed buildings', the purpose of which is not known.[3] An abstract of title to the Cobham Park estate recites that in September 1773 the premises were in the occupation of Messrs Raby and Mereton, iron masters. In 1777 Raby joined forces with Obadiah Wix Rogers of Bermondsey to develop another site at nearby Coxes Lock at Addlestone.[4]

Domesday Book had recorded three mills on the River Mole at Cobham. These were at Cobham, Ashford (on Cobham Tilt) and Downside. The mill at Downside had been used for the production of paper since the early eighteenth century and was for a long time owned by the Hillyer family. Surviving land tax assessments for Cobham commence in 1780 and then show Downside mill still owned by the Hillyer family but occupied by Raby. In 1783 Raby is recorded as both owner and occupier.

By 1781 Downside Mill was described as comprising one messuage, two shops, one stable, one iron mill, two forges, three gardens, four acres of land four acres of meadow, one acre of common pasture, free fishing on the River Mole, and a rent of £40 per annum.[5]

The whereabouts of Raby's residence in the Cobham district is still something of a mystery. This is not helped by a nineteenth century historian of Llanelli, where Raby settled after leaving Cobham, writing that Raby sold Cobham Park in Surrey and brought the purchase money – £175,000 – to Wales about 1795.[6] Unfortunately this oft-repeated story has become part of the legend of the founding of modern-day Llanelli! In fact, Raby never owned Cobham Park although he may have lived there for a short time. A land tax receipt dated 15 March 1800, which is held with the Cobham Park deeds, states that the mansion house and pleasure grounds; the park, canal, meadows and Trusslers Field; the new allotments in the late enclosures; the farm etc, were all then in the occupation of Alexander Raby.

However, it is possible that the confusion here has arisen through the fact that 'Cobham Park' was in Raby's time an area of land holding as opposed to a building.[7] The mansion house, now known as Cobham Park, was then known as Downe Place. It had been built in the early part of the eighteenth century on the site of a previous house. The eighteenth-century mansion was, in turn, replaced in 1870 by the present building, which was designed by E M Barry.[8]

In the middle of the eighteenth century, Field Marshall Lord Ligonier, Commander in Chief of the British Army, purchased Downe Place. On his death in 1770 the property passed to his nephew Edward who became the second Earl Ligonier. It was during this noble lord's occupation of Downe Place that a scandalous affair took place between his wife and the Italian poet Alfieri.[9] Following the death of Edward Ligonier, in 1782 Henry Lawes Luttrell, Earl of Carhampton, purchased the estate. It was Carhampton who had fought John 'Liberty' Wilkes in the infamous Middlesex by-election in 1769.

The 'Plan of Cobham Mills Belonging to Alex. Raby, Esq.' reproduced on the cover of this volume, which possibly dates from the 1790s, shows a substantial house close to the iron works. A detail is shown in figure 1. This property had its own pleasure grounds as well as stables, laundry, and a 'cold bath'. However, land tax assessments for the neighbouring parish of Stoke D'Abernon for the period 1784–1792 show Raby as then occupying an unnamed property forming part of Sir Francis Vincent's Stoke Manor estate. Additionally, the Stoke parish registers record the burial of Alexander, son of Alexander and Ann Raby, on 6 July 1776. This may have been the child who was baptised at Cobham in 1774. Another son, also named Alexander, seems to have born shortly after this, in 1778. Other Raby baptisms that can be traced in the Cobham registers are Margaret Maria (1772) Catherine (1775) Arthur Turnour (1791).

A possible reason for Raby and his family choosing to live at Stoke D'Abernon may have been the fact that Josiah Wedgwood II lived at Stoke Manor House between 1779 and about 1800. Coleridge the poet recorded a visit there in 1798.[10] It is possible that Raby introduced Wedgwood to the area. Raby remained close to the Wedgwood family and seems to have borrowed heavily from them.[11]

From 1793 onwards the Stoke land tax assessments name the property as 'Ashford'. I once assumed this to be Ashford Farm House, a substantial building dating from mediaeval times, standing close to the River Mole at Upper Tilt, Cobham, which was owned from 1782 to 1828 by Edward White, a wealthy Cobham farmer.[12] It would have been a very convenient place for the enterprising Raby to live, with easy access to the mill by fording the river and following the bridle path over the adjoining fields. However, a 1794 plan of an abortive

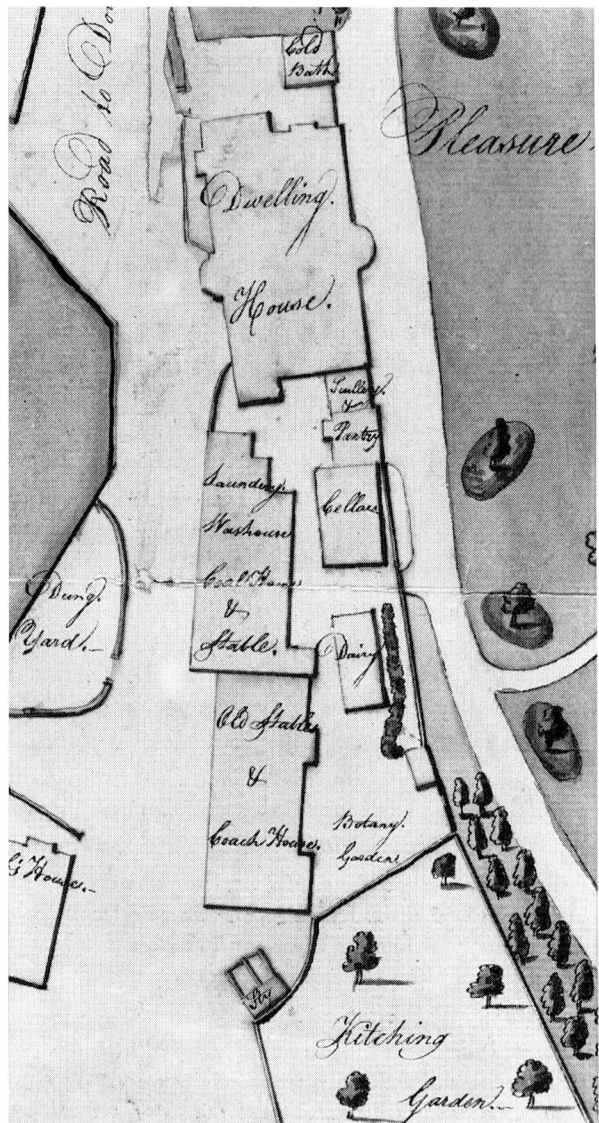

Figure 1. Detail from the Plan of Cobham Mills Belonging to Alex. Raby, Esq., showing the dwelling house, its outbuildings and part of the pleasure grounds. (See also cover illustration).

proposal for a navigable canal from Fetcham to the Thames (figure 2)[13] shows that Ashford Farm (31 and 32 on the plan) was owned by Edward White and occupied by Robert Sink. Two adjoining pieces of land contiguous with Ashford Farm but slightly to the south-west (both numbered 33 on the plan) were owned by Sir Francis Vincent and occupied by Alexander Raby and they can be safely identified with the property referred to in the land tax. The Stoke D'Abernon tithe map of 1846 and the 1869 Ordnance Survey map show a small building in this area. Whatever stood here must have been very close to the site of the present railway station and its former goods yards (now a car park). Presumably, the site was cleared and levelled when the new Waterloo to Guildford line was constructed in 1885.

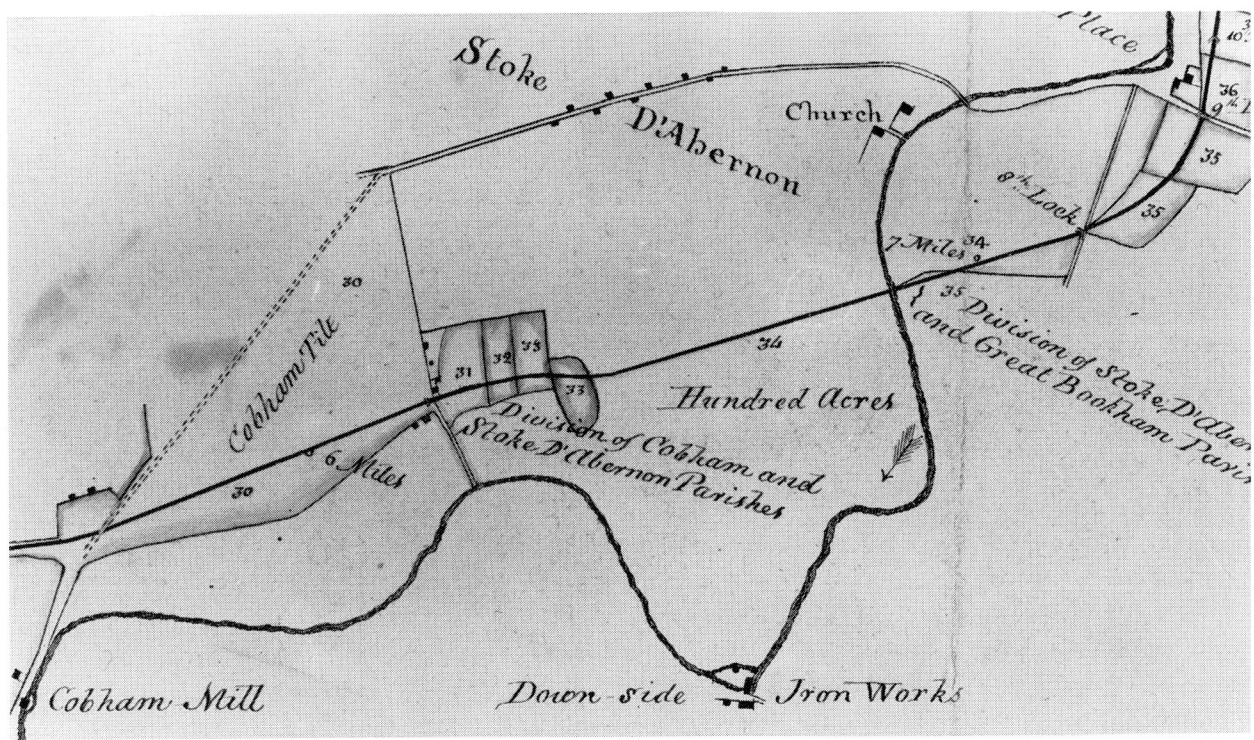

Copyright of Surrey History Service

Figure 2 Detail of A plan of the intended navigable canal from near Fetcham Corn Mill in the Parish of Fetcham to the River Thames near Walton in the County of Surrey. Surveyed in 1794 by Charles Robert. Reproduced at the original scale of 20 chains (440 yards) to 1 inch. The left-to-right orientation of the map is approximately NNW–SSE. The detail shows Cobham Mill and Downside Iron Works on the River Mole. The proposed route of the canal passes through plots 33 occupied by Alexander Raby and then across a section of Cobham Tilt allotted to Raby under the Cobham Enclosure Awards. Reproduced by permission of Surrey History Service (SHC: QS6/8/3/1).

The 1869 OS map indicates a right of way running from Ashford Farm House, through the site once occupied by Raby and across the Hundred Acres to Downside Mill. This raises the question of whether Raby actually lived here or whether he used it for housing workers from the mill.

The 1794 canal map raises other interesting points. In 1793 there had been a proposal to construct a canal 'from the Coast of Sussex to Horsham from thence to Dorking and by means of the River Mole thro' Mickleham Leatherhead Cobham etc etc and so on to the River Thames'. William Abington of Leigh Hill House Cobham claimed that almost everyone from Dorking to the Thames was strongly opposed to it.[14]

The canal proposed in 1794 would have crossed the land occupied by Raby before cutting through part of Ashford Farm. It would then have crossed Cobham Tilt in a south-westerly direction towards Leigh Hill. It is difficult to believe that the entrepreneurial Raby did not have a commercial interest of some sort in a major enterprise such as this proposal. Unfortunately, no documentary evidence to support this seems to have survived. However, the fact that the straight line of the canal would have had to make a very slight detour to run through the two pieces of land which Raby rented from Sir Francis Vincent fuels the speculation.

To the facts already mentioned, it should be added that under the 1793 enclosure of Cobham's commons, Raby was allotted a very long narrow strip of land that ran right across the middle of the old Tilt Common almost from Ashford Farm to the beginning of Leigh Hill Road. Why was he allotted this strange-shaped piece of land whose only access was at either end? Did Raby plan that this should be used for the proposed canal? Raby was no stranger to canals and sometime during his time at Downside Mill, he had diverted the River Mole through a cut which he made across the Hundred Acres. This is referred to in a letter to the agent of Harvey Combe of Cobham Park.[15] Did Raby propose linking his iron mills with this new canal? Sadly, in the absence of documentary evidence we can only guess at what Raby might have had in mind. Letters in the Wedgwood archive reveal Raby's later involvement in the Monmouth Canal.

Returning to the land at Stoke, by 1805 Ashford is shown in the land tax as belonging to Hugh Smith, who had purchased the manor of Stoke

D'Abernon from the Vincent family, and the occupier is George Freeland. However 'Part of the Hundred Acres' remained occupied by Raby and, the following year, this land is shown as being in the occupation of a Mr Bunn,[16] and he in 1810 was replaced by Jackson & Co., the new owners of Downside Mill.

Unfortunately, nothing is known about the impact of Raby and his iron works at Downside Mill upon the local community. At Coxes Lock Raby had installed a 'great hammer' nicknamed Hackering Jack which delivered some 2,700 blows an hour. It could be heard in nearby Weybridge, where local landowners and residents lodged objections to the noise and a feud developed between them and Raby's Company.[17] Did the residents of Cobham have to suffer similar inconveniences?

There must have been a dramatic increase in traffic on the local lanes as plant and raw material were delivered to Downside and the finished products were taken away. A plan of the mills in Raby's time indicates substantial stabling for horses and ponies. The replacement of the old wooden bridge over the Mole between Cobham and Downside in 1787 by a new a brick structure, designed by George Gwilt, was to Raby's great advantage. He would have had a personal interest in the provision of new and improved roads brought about by the enclosures, no doubt greatly assisted by his position as parish surveyor of highways between 1786 and 1794, and his probable involvement in proposals for a canal has already been mentioned.

Raby's active role in the enclosure of the common fields at Cobham in 1793 has already been mentioned. He claimed rights for himself in respect of the following:

> Downside Mill, with about Eight Acres of Land belonging to it;
> A Field known by the Name of the Old Meadow – Eight Acres.
> A Field near Lord Ligoniers Gates – One Acre & a Quarter.
> A Small piece of Land bought of Mr Page on which I have built two Cottages – about 1/3 Acres.

The claim to the Enclosure Commissioners submitted by the Trustees in respect of Downe Place included:

> Part of Down Farm &c, with Farm House, Barns & Other Buildings, thereto belonging, also Cobham Park, Hanford Meadow, & some Plowing Land, with Barn & Other Buildings, thereto belonging, Rented by Mr. Alex. Raby.

> A Cottage called Hawthorn, also a ditto formerly belonging to a small Farm rented by Mr Raby for his workmen.

Around this time Raby was showing interest in the coalfield at Llanelli in South Wales and in 1796 he took over the iron foundry and furnace at what is now called Furnace.[18] However Raby continued to maintain the works in Cobham and elsewhere in Surrey. As late as 1803/4 he built a row of model cottages for his workers overlooking Downside Common. These cottages were built on land which Raby acquired by exchange from Lord Carhampton in 1803. The 1805 land tax assessments show them as being occupied by 'workers'. Raby sold the cottages to William Moss of Cobham in 1809. Originally known as Tin Row and then as Tinmans Row, the terrace remains today as a rare example of early industrial workers' cottages, as illustrated in figure 3.[19]

In 1805 Lord Carhampton sold Cobham Park (as the mansion house and estate had then become known) to Harvey Christian Combe.[20] In 1822 the Combe family's agent had evidently written to Raby requesting details of the alterations he had made to the course of the Mole during his time at Downside. Raby replied with a three-page letter, a copy of which has survived among the Cobham Park papers. It seems that Harvey Combe's son, also named Harvey, was considering the construction of another weir, possibly to build up a head of water to maintain the lake at Cobham Park.

Raby's letter provides a detailed account of his work in trying to maintain the necessary head of water to ensure that the mill ran efficiently.[21] He writes of how he had constructed a tumbling bay in the river:

> I put Eight Flashes about 18 in deep and raised Banks on each side of the River to prevent its overflowing the Meadows on each side. I very soon found we were very much flooded in the Winter. I then (the next Spring) begun to drive up a Level from Ashford to our Mill to enable me so to do I purchased the Islands and also Lucy's Mill[22] which sold again and drove the level up into the Mill Tail from the Island. Finding still we were very much flooded I agreed with Sir Francis Vincent to let me make the Cut across the 100 acres when that was done I did not find its good effects sufficiently useful without preventing the stream from the Mill and that from the floodgates joining so soon as they did in flood time they still came back upon me so as stop our Wheels in heavy floods. I then made a dam across the River at the upper end of the 12 acres across to the 100

Figure 3. Tinmans Row, Downside Common, photographed in 1997. The row of workers' cottages was built by Alexander Raby in 1803–1804.

acres and turned all our working water down what was called the Old River so that the two streams did not join till where the old River emptys itself into the Corn Mill Head and by thus separating the two streams we were never after flooded but whether we had a legal right to put the Dam across just at the upper end of the 12 acres or not I wont pretend to say only that no person offered to stop me and at the entrance into the Old River there was across the mouth of it several upright posts that gave it the appearance of having formerly had floodgates there.

Raby concluded this letter with a nice personal touch, which allows us a glimpse of his life at Cobham:

I am as well as ever tho I cannot run as fast not jump as high as when Ld. Tankerville, Sir Francis Vincent, his brother and we used to play at Cricket upon the Tilt 50 years ago. But thank God we are as well as we are. Send me a little Cobham news when you write again.[23]

By 1806 Raby was getting into financial difficulties in Wales and in June 1807 he was forced to convene a meeting of creditors. It was probably these events that led him to consider the sale of the works at Downside. In preparation for the sale Raby had to clarify his title to his Cobham properties and on 27 February 1806 he executed a lease from Hugh Smith of Stoke House of eight acres of land, river banks and water courses for 99 years from Michaelmas 1805 at £60 per annum, 'together with the free use of the cut or canal made by the said Alexander Raby through the said 8 acres, and also the use of the banks raised by the said Alexander Raby on the north-east side of the said River Mole aforesaid in the said meadow called the 100 acres for the purpose of impounding and raising the water his mill in order to benefit and give additional fore to the works carried on there'.[24]

According to an abstract of title with the Cobham Park deeds, the sale to John Bunn appears to have taken place on 13 June 1806.[25] At this time the iron works consisted of the following:

All those several mill houses, iron mills, presses, erections and together with the said piece or parcel of ground or yard whereon the said mill, forges and other buildings were erected, containing by estimation 1 acre 1 rood and 30 perches and together with the cottage commonly called the Blacksmiths Cottage erected on part thereof adjoining to the floodgate, and garden occupied therewith, containing together by estimation one acre one rood and 36 perches and which said last mentioned piece or parcel of land together with two other pieces or parcels of land or ground then converted into and used as a yard and on part of which said mills forges and other erections and buildings were erected, were formerly called or known by the name of the Wharf.

There were also 'works, wheels, engines and locks, pipes, fixtures, tools, implements, apparatus, copper boiler, shafts, forges, cylenders, harness, waggons, horses.[26] The increasing use of steam-powered machinery and the need to be near the source of raw materials meant that Downside could no longer be considered as a viable place to operate an iron forge. In 1809, the mill was being advertised for sale in *The Times* newspaper:

> Cobham Iron Works, Surrey – By Messrs Sharp and Kirkup, at Garraway's on Friday, May 12, at 12 o'clock, by order of the proprietors, dissolving partnership (unless an acceptable offer be previously made by private contract).
>
> A Capital Freehold Estate, comprising those valuable and extensive premises, the Cobham Iron Works, situate on the River Mole, with an excellent and very commodious Family residence, stabling for 20 horses, offices of ever useful description, and about 14 acres of land (of which 7 are leasehold, for 96 years, at a very low rent), the works are most complete and extensive, and constantly adapted from a fine head of water, of 11 feet fall, not subject to floods; are particularly adapted for the concern now carried on; and likewise for copper or wire works, powder, oil, paper, or corn mills on a large scale. They comprise a capital iron mill, two large anchorsmith's shops (one adapted for a mill), an iron foundry, a forge, and three smith's shops. A coke oven, counting-houses, warehouses, and a very convenient dwellinghouse for a superintendent of the works; the machinery is in perfect order, and constructed on the most approved principles. May be viewed one month previous to the sale on Mondays and Saturdays, with tickets only, which with particulars maybe had of Messrs Sharp and Kirkup, Winchester-street, where plans of the estate may be seen.[27]

In 1810 Downside Mill was in the ownership of Jackson & Co.[28] By 1814 the iron mill had been dismantled. On 29 October 1818 the property was sold by John Hunter and William Bell of Bishops Wearmouth, Durham, merchants, and John Jackson of Dowgate Wharf, London, ironmonger, to Thomas Mellor of Southwark, horsehair manufacturer. The deeds recite that the mill had been in the occupation of Raby 'afterwards of John Bunn late of the said John Jackson now of the said Thomas Mellor'.

Thomas Mellor used Downside as a flock or rag mill. By 1865 when Downside Mill was again advertised for sale, most of Raby's buildings had disappeared. By the time of the 1871 census the mill was being used as a saw mill occupied by John Wood, timber merchant and builder. Later that century, the mill resumed its more intimate connection with Cobham Park when a wheel was installed for generating electricity. During the twentieth century the mill has been used for a variety of industrial purposes and is now also used for office accommodation.

Notes and References

1. Alexander Raby – A Surrey Ironmaster: G E Buttriss (unpublished manuscript).
2. *The Reading Mercury*, 30 April 1770.
3. Painshill Park Trust: copies of Hamilton's accounts. I am grateful to Mrs Mavis Collier, Honorary Archivist of the Trust, for providing this information.
4. See Barker, this volume, page 30.
5. Greenwood, G, *The Elmbridge Water Mills* (typescript, 1980), 19–21, quoting Walker, T E C, Cobham: Manorial History, *Surrey Archaeological Collections*, **58** (1961), 47–78 at 62.
6. Innes, J, *Old Llanelly* (1904).
7. The land holdings rented by Raby for which the trustees of Downe Place claimed rights under the enclosure awards include 'Also Cobham Park' as distinct from 'the Mansion House'.
8. Taylor, D C, *The Book of Cobham* (Barracuda Books, 1982); Taylor, D C, *Cobham Houses and their Occupants* (Cobham, Appleton Publications, 1999), 43–52.
9. Taylor, D C, *Cobham Characters* (Cobham, Appleton Publications, 1998), 17–25.
10. *Ibid*, 36–9.
11. John Potter noted in discussion that the Buttriss-held papers included copies of correspondence from Josiah Wedgwood relating to Raby's debts: Univ. Keele Library Documents: 18984-26, 6 Feb 1793; 1534-2 undated; 1531-2, 28 Sept 1797; 1544-2, 3 April 1804(?).
12. Taylor, *Cobham Houses*, ref. 8, 1–4.
13. Surrey History Centre (SHC): QS6/8/3/1–2.
14. Archives of St. George's Chapel, Windsor: XVII, 33, 17, and quoted in Walker, Cobham: Manorial History, 78.
15. Quoted on page 18 of this paper.
16. This must have been John Bunn of John Bunn & Co., Hoop and iron Merchants, of Dowgate Wharf, London. In 1808 Bunn had taken over Ham Haw or Thames Lock Mill, Weybridge, from where he issued his own token coinage (illustrated in Potter, this volume, page 9). From papers in Mr Combe's possession it seems that Bunn acquired Downside Mill from Raby and then sold it on to John Jackson.
17. See Barker, this volume, pages 31, 32.
18. It is possible that Raby's introduction to Wales was through Francis Lloyd, MP for Montgomeryshire (1795–1799), who had married Elizabeth Graham, granddaughter of John, 1st Earl Ligonier, and who was one of the trustees of the Cobham Park estate after Edward Ligonier's death. For details of Raby's work at Llanelli, see John, this volume, pages 35–40.
19. Taylor, *Cobham Houses*, ref. 8, 169–70.
20. Combe, a friend of the Prince of Wales and Charles James Fox, had made his fortune in porter brewing and was Lord Mayor of London in 1799 and MP for the City in 1802.
21. Photocopy in possession of the author.

22. It was in 1788 that Raby acquired 'Lucy's Mill' at Cobham. Thomas Lucy had been the Cobham miller whose questionable claim to a share in the estates of the Lucy family of Charlecote is told in Taylor, ref. 9, 13–16.
23. *The Gazetteer & London Daily Advertiser*, 24 August 1771: 'On Monday next will be played on Cobham-tilt, the second great cricket-match for 20l. between the Earl of Tankerville and the Cobham-club, against – Vaughan, Esq; and the Dorking club, who won the first match, with only three wickets down, in their last hands.' The Earl of Tankerville who lived at Mount Felix, Walton on Thames, helped established the rules for modern cricket in 1774.
24. Cobham Park Estate Papers: 27 February 1806 : Lease : Smith to Raby.
25. An estate map dated 1807 (SHC: 2610/38/21), which shows the iron mill still in Raby's possession, appears to be from the 1790s. It does not show Tinman's row (built 1803/4) and a number of the landowners shown are not those of 1807. It is similar to the Cobham enclosure map and may be a slightly updated copy of this.
26. Walker, ref. 5, 62–3.
27. *The Times*, 8 May 1809.
28. SHC: Cobham land tax.

Downside Mill, Cobham

ALAN CROCKER

This paper provides a summary of the history of Downside Mill from pre-Conquest times to the present day. However, the account of the period when Alexander Raby was active at the site is given in more detail. In particular, an attempt has been made to interpret relevant documentary information in terms of the industrial processes which Raby is likely to have used. For example, the detailed plan of the mill reproduced on the cover of this volume is examined and compared both with later maps and the surviving structures and watercourses on the site.

Downside Mill, formerly known as Down Mill, stands on the left bank of the River Mole approximately 2 km south-east of Cobham parish church and 1 km east of the settlement of Downside. Its site (TQ 118 583), as indicated in figure 1, appears to have been selected to be at the confluence of a small stream which runs from the south and the much larger Mole which comes from the east before flowing away to the north. These watercourses must have formed the original parish boundaries between Cobham, Stoke D'Abernon and Little Bookham. However, the creation of the mill, probably in the Anglo-Saxon period, and later developments have resulted in the formation of new water channels and the blocking of others. As a result there appear to have been local changes in the boundaries and the mill buildings are now entirely in Cobham parish.

Before Alexander Raby

An outline of the history of Downside Mill before it was acquired by Alexander Raby in 1770 is provided in table 1.

The mill was probably one of the three mills recorded at Cobham in the Domesday survey of 1086 but it is not mentioned by name. The first specific reference is in 1331 when the tenants of Down manor made an annual payment of nine gallons of honey to Chertsey Abbey for allowing them to grind their corn at Down's own mill. Then in 1565 Thomas Lyfield, lord of the manor of Stoke D'Abernon, and his wife Frances agreed to allow Thomas a Down of Cobham to repair and operate Down Mill, which had been owned by Down's ancestors and was now decayed. Likewise in 1720 an agreement was reached between Viscountess Lanesborough of Down Place (now Cobham Park) and Thomas Morris the tenant of the mill about flooding meadows to fertilise the soil. This agreement shows that the property included 'a messuage or tenement, mill houses, paper mills and corn mills, commonly called Downe Mills'.[1]

The fact that paper was made at the mill in 1720 suggests that earlier records of papermakers in Cobham parish registers in 1687 and 1694 also relate to Down Mill. Again an inventory dated 1691 of the property of John Bicknell, late of the parish of Cobham deceased, includes raw materials and equipment for making paper, which indicates that he too was probably at the mill. In 1728 Thomas Hillier (Hillyer), a papermaker, devised to Richard Hinton a dwelling house and paper mills in Cobham for 11 years. Unfortunately, in 1733, the mill house and paper mill were burned down but the mill was rebuilt within six months as Mary Hillier, widow of Thomas, insured her new-built

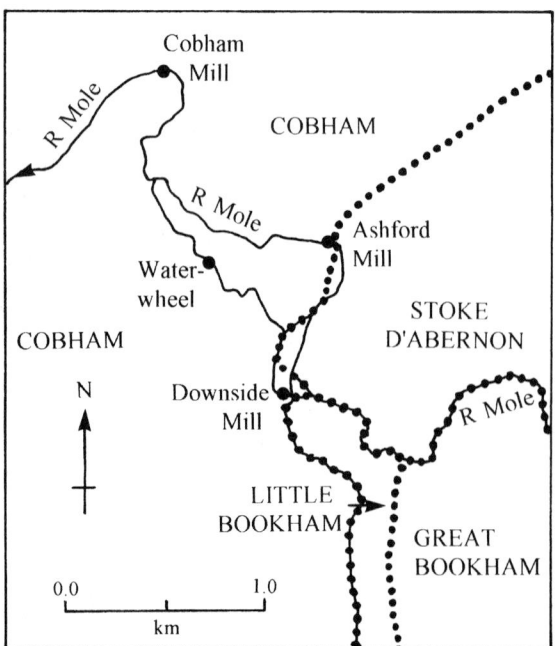

Figure 1. Sketch map showing the locations of Downside, Ashford and Cobham Mills, a waterwheel in Cobham Park, the River Mole and other watercourses as they are today, and the parish boundaries between Cobham, Stoke D'Abernon, Little Bookham and Great Bookham.

Table 1. Brief chronology of Downside Mill before its acquisition by Alexander Raby

1086	Domesday: 3 [corn] watermills at Cobham, valued at 13s 4d
1331	Tenants of Down manor grind their corn at Down Mill
1565	Agreement to repair and operate the decayed Down Mill
1687	Wm Berrey (Borroy?), papermaker, in Cobham parish registers
1691	Property of John Bicknell: rags, moulds, deckles and paper
1694	John Meers, papermaker in Cobham parish registers
1720	Corn & paper mills. Thos Morris tenant, previously John Garton
1728	Thos Hillier devises paper mill to Richard Hinton
1733	House and paper mill destroyed by fire – arson suspected
1733	Mary Hillier insures new paper mill, occupied by Richard Hinton
1735	John Hillier, papermaker
1749	John Hillier insures rag houses etc
1752	Elizabeth Hunt from paper mills in parish registers
1766	Will of John Hillier, bookseller, proved 1769
1770	Joseph Hunt, papermaker, dealer, etc, bankrupt; mill for sale

Table 2. Brief chronology of Downside Mill during its occupation by Alexander Raby

1770	Lease acquired by Alexander Raby and Mr Mereton, a banker.
1773	Mill in occupation of Raby & Mereton, iron masters
1780	Mill still owned by Hillier (Hillyer) family
1781	Mill has 1 messuage, 2 shops, 1 iron mill, 2 forges; rent £40 pa
1783	Raby both owner and occupier of Downside Mill
1798c	Plan of Cobham [Downside] Mills belonging to Alexander Raby
1800	Downe Place house in Cobham Park in occupation of Raby
1803	Raby builds Tinmans Row – cottages at Downside Common
1806	Raby sells his iron works at Downside to John Bunn
1809	Raby sells Tinmans Row

paper mill called Downe Mills in the occupation of Richard Hinton. However in 1735 Mary's son John Hillier was the papermaker. He continued until at least 1749 but in his will of 1766 he is described as a bookseller of Cobham. Meanwhile in 1752 Elizabeth Hunt of the paper mills is mentioned in the parish registers and in 1770 Joseph Hunt papermaker, dealer and chapman was bankrupt and Downside Mill was for sale.[2] Incidentally the 1720 agreement is the last known reference to corn milling on the site.

Occupation by Alexander Raby

As a result of the sale of Downside Mill in 1770, Alexander Raby and Mr Mereton, who was a London banker, acquired the lease. An account of what is known from documentary sources about Raby from this time until he finally left Cobham in 1809 has already been given by Taylor (pages 15–21). The main facts are summarised in table 2.

The most detailed information is provided by the 'Plan of Cobham Mills belonging to Alexander Raby Esq.' which is reproduced as the cover of this volume. The map is undated, has north at the bottom and was drawn at a scale of 1:480 (1 inch to 40 feet). It is on a trimmed sheet of handmade paper measuring 393 × 306 mm, which is consistent with foolscap. This displays the watermark I TAYLOR with Britannia showing that it was made by John Taylor who was at Basted Mill at Wrotham in Kent from 1776 to 1802 when he died[3] and also at Carshalton Mill in Surrey in 1777.[4] In 1794 it became financially advantageous for papermakers to include the year in the watermark[5] but no date is present in this case so the paper is probably earlier. This need not however be inconsistent with the unauthenticated claim that the plan dates from about 1798,[6] as the draughtsman may not have used recently made paper.

A redrawn version of Raby's plan is shown in figure 2, the buildings and other features being numbered and described in the caption. In addition, a detail of the original, showing the two water-powered buildings, is reproduced as figure 3. It seems likely that the mill 22, with a waterwheel on each side, the copper foundry 23, and the nearby dwelling house 49 correspond with the earlier buildings associated with the paper mills. It is suggested here that 22 was a roller mill used by Raby for producing thin sheets of iron and copper. This would have required a substantial brick building and would probably have been new as the old paper mill would have consisted mainly of a timber drying loft. The adjacent copper foundry was presumably used for casting bars to be rolled into sheet copper ready for converting, for example, into kitchen pans.

The largest building, with three waterwheels, is the complex 13–18, housing a women's shop, cutting house, break house, tilt, forge and iron foundry

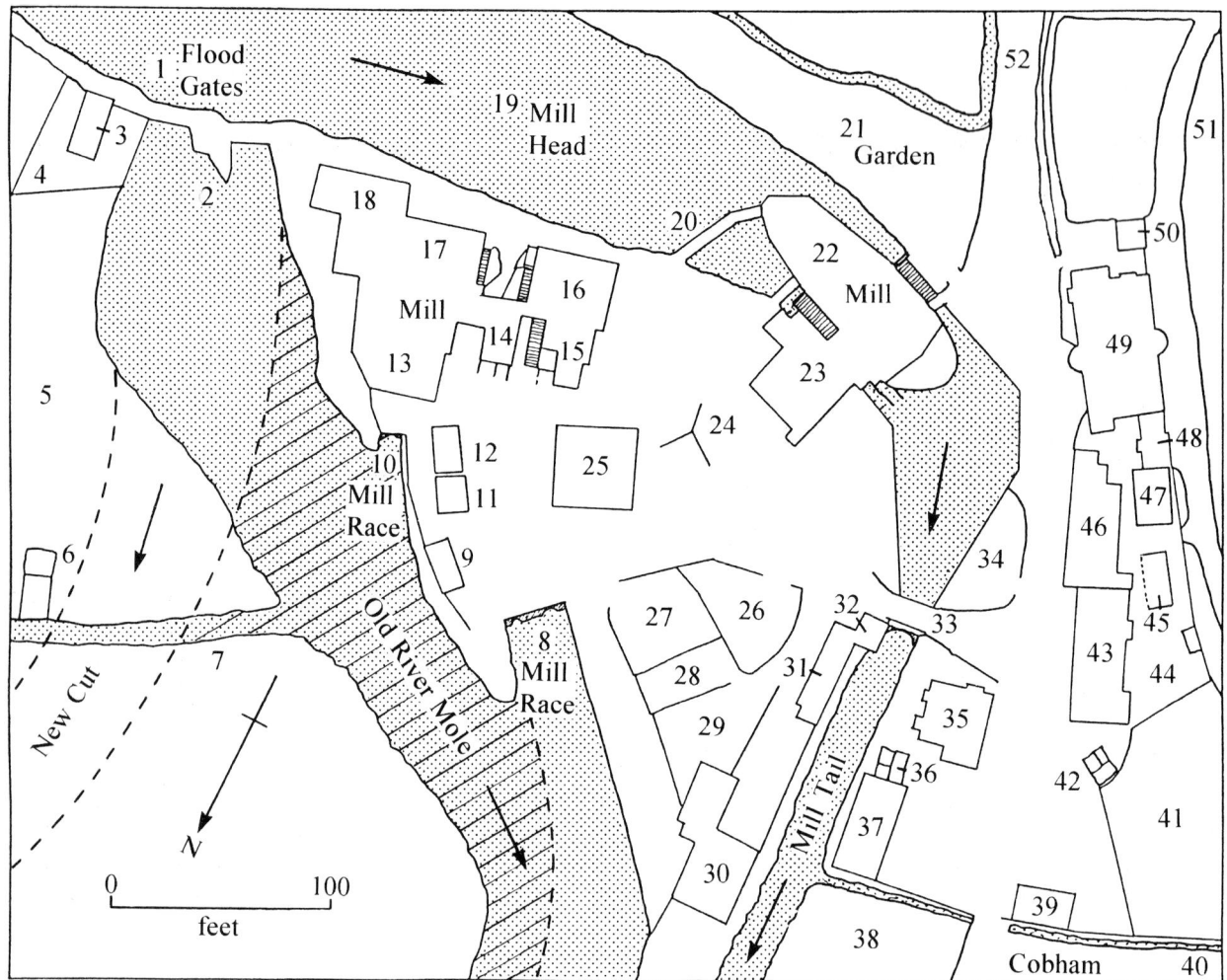

Figure 2. Plan of Downside Mills redrawn from the Plan of Cobham Mills belonging to Alexander Raby Esq., reproduced on the cover of this volume. The original is thought to date from about 1798. The notation, using the original spelling, is as follows: 1. Floodgates; 2. Flood Gate Hole; 3. Standen's House; 4. Garden; 5. Dog Kennell Field; 6. Dog Kennell; 7. Flash Race; 8. Forge & Tilt Race; 9. Brick & Lime House; 10. Cylinder Race; 11. Helve House; 12. Smoak House; 13. Women's Shop; 14. Cutting House; 15. Break House; 16. Tilt; 17. Forge; 18. Iron Foundery; 19. Mill Head; 20. Bridge; 21. Mill Garden; 22. Mill; 23. Copper Foundery; 24. Triangles; 25. Coak House; 26. Coak Penn; 27. Charcoal Penn; 28. Charcoal Penn; 29. Coal Penn; 30. Smith's Shop; 31. Counting House & Assay Office &c; 32. Ware House; 33. Bridge; 34. Dung Yard; 35. Gibb's House; 36. Sty; 37. New Stables & Coach House; 38. Marsh Meadow; 39. Carpenter's Shop; 40. Road to Cobham; 41. Kitching Garden; 42. Sty; 43. Old Stables & Coach House; 44. Botany Garden; 45. Dairy; 46. Laundry, Washouse, Coal House & Stable; 47. Cellars; 48. Scullery & Pantry; 49. Dwelling House; 50. Cold Bath; 51. Pleasure Ground; 52. Road to Down Farm. The broken lines at the left show, approximately, the route of the new cut, constructed by Raby after the plan was drawn. At the same time the shaded section of the original River Mole was filled resulting in a narrower forge and tilt race.

respectively. It appears to have been built by Alexander Raby on newly constructed water channels and was clearly the heart of his iron mill. It would have contained furnaces for melting pig iron, which required bellows or pistons in cylinders to provide blasts of air, tilt hammers for removing slag from the iron and for shaping it into bars and shears for cutting iron bars and plates.[7] The tail-water from the waterwheels passed underground to the forge and tilt race 8 and the cylinder race 10. The iron foundry would presumably have been used for both large objects such as anchors and smaller pieces of ironmongery. The women's shop 13 is at first surprising as women did not normally work at iron mills. However, in 1803 Raby built 'Tinmans Row' 1 km to the west of the mill on Downside Common,[8] which suggests that cast iron objects or plates were being coated with tin at the mill. The iron had to be thoroughly cleaned before being dipped in molten tin and this work was carried out by women. Iron bars could readily be taken across the bridge 20 to the mill 22 for rolling and the resulting sheets, together with cast objects and copper sheets, returned for tinning. Building 13–18 has

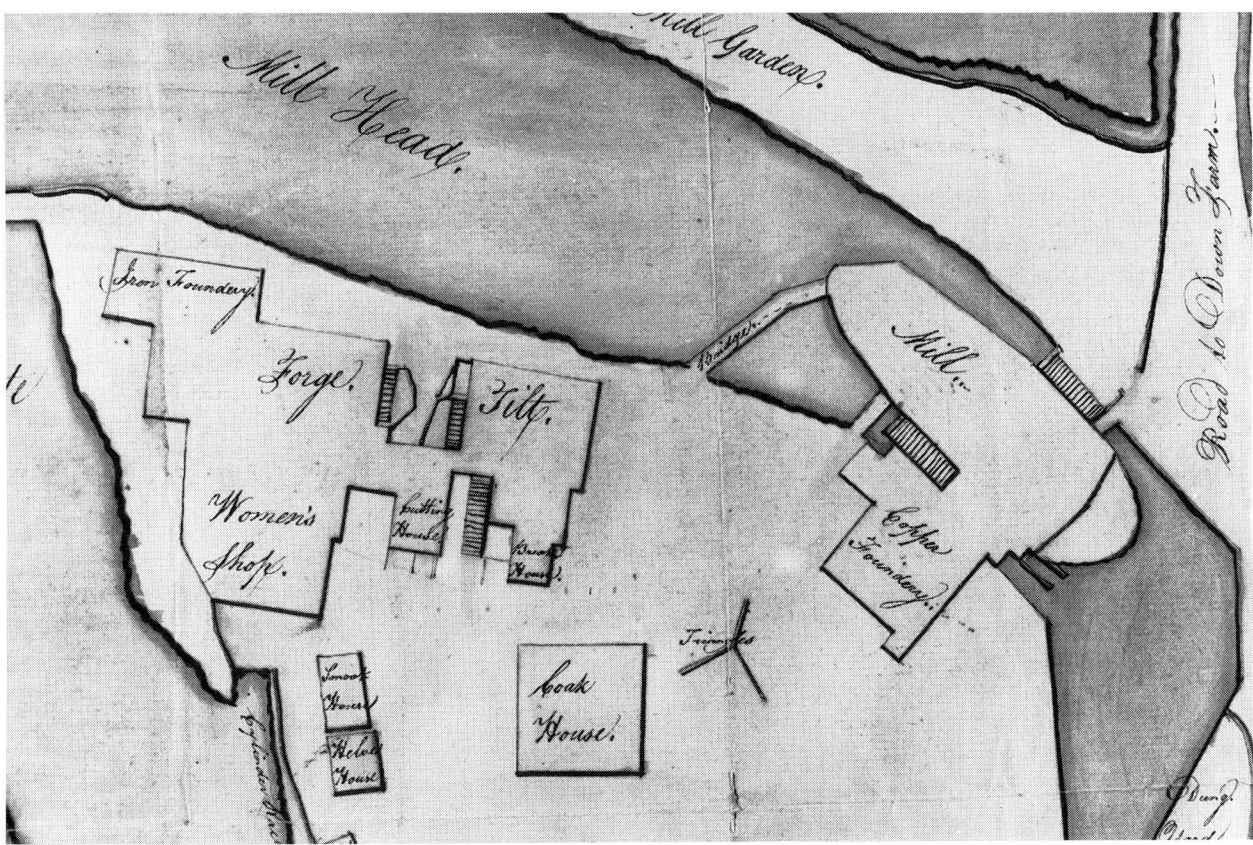

Figure 3. Reduced detail (× 0.83) of the Plan of Cobham Mills belonging to Alex. Raby Esq. thought to date from about 1798. It shows, primarily, the two water-powered mill buildings. The full plan is reproduced in colour on the cover of this volume and has been redrawn in figure 2.

a very complicated outline and appears therefore to have developed gradually over many years rather than being built at one time. This suggests that the Raby plan dates from towards the end of his occupation of the site.

Another interesting building is the coke house 25 which could have been a kiln for producing coke from small or pulverised coal. As Downside Mill was a forge and not a furnace, the coke would not have been used for smelting. However it is interesting that at that time the best quality tin plate was produced from pig iron refined using charcoal furnaces whereas cheaper tin plate, known as 'coke plate' was refined using coke furnaces.[9] Adjacent to the coke house is feature 24 labelled triangles, which could have been where the coke was left to cool after being taken from the kiln. Also the brick and lime house 9 could have been a store for materials needed to maintain the kiln. The smoke house 12 might also be related to the coke house but the adjoining helve house 11 was presumably a store for spare shafts or helves for the tilt hammers. The coal and charcoal which were brought to the site and the manufactured coke were stored in pens 26–29 between the coke house and the two smith's shops 30. There is also a large dung yard 34 not far from the dwelling house 49 and Gibb's house 35. Perhaps it is not surprising that, with the din from the trip hammers, the smoke from the coke kilns, the nauseous stench from grease and suet covering the molten tin and the smell of the dung, Raby and his wife do not seem to have lived in the dwelling house for very long.[10]

The above explanation and interpretation has not unfortunately resolved the problem of dating the Raby plan but other sources of information help. In 1822 Raby wrote a letter explaining how he had altered the watercourses around Downside Mill.[11] In order to interpret this information available large scale nineteenth century maps have been consulted and the sketch map of figure 4 is based on these. First, Raby states that he raised the level of the water upstream from his mill to Brays Mill, by which he meant Slyfield corn mill (TQ 133 578) which in 1776 and again in 1808 was occupied by Henry Bray.[12] To do this he states that he placed flashes or boards 18 inches deep on the tumbling bay or sluice marked A in figure 4 and raised the banks on each side of the river to avoid flooding the meadows. This would have provided a much

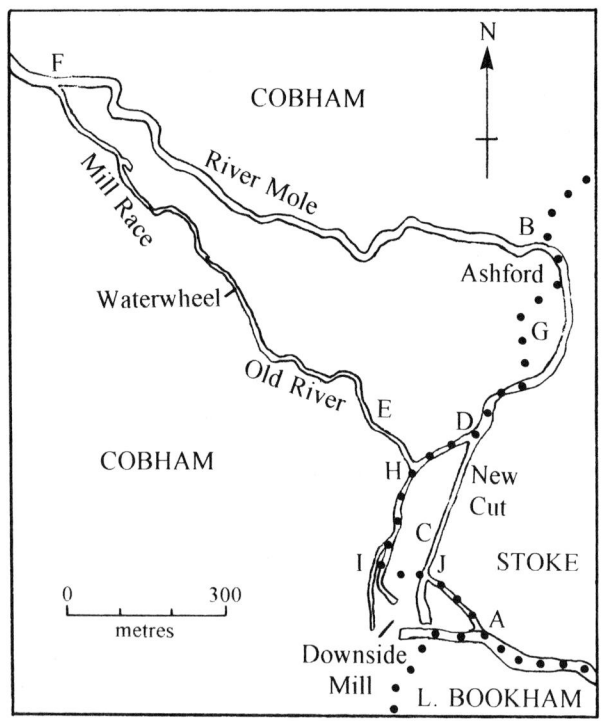

Figure 4. Sketch map of the watercourses near Downside Mill which were altered by Alexander Raby. The parish boundaries between Cobham, Stoke D'Abernon and Little Bookham are indicated; the code letters A to J are explained in the text.

larger reservoir of water for his mill and would have increased the available water power by about one-sixth. However, he soon discovered that the mill was 'very much flooded in the winter'. So, the following spring, according to his letter, he levelled the river from the mill-tail downstream to Ashford, marked B in figure 4. This would also have had the effect of increasing the head of water and hence the power available at Downside Mill. To do the work Raby says that he had to purchase some land and, rather surprisingly, Lucy's Mill. However, he sold this property again when the work was completed. Thomas Lucy was the tenant of Cobham Mill (TQ 111 599) in 1772, purchased it in 1778 and insured it a year later but by 1787 John Tupper was the miller.[13] Also the land tax records[14] show that Raby owned Cobham Mill in 1788 but did not twelve months later. It appears therefore that he carried out this work on the watercourses in 1787–88 or shortly before.

Unfortunately Raby's levelling work did not prevent the mill from being flooded. So, he agreed with Sir Francis Vincent, who owned the 100 acres field east of Downside Mill to make the artificial straight cut, marked C in figure 4, across the western edge of this field. However, although the separate water channels from the mill and from the flood gates did not now merge for some 350 metres below the mill, in time of flood the water still backed-up to the mill and stopped the waterwheels from turning. Therefore Raby constructed a dam at D which diverted the tail water from the mill down 'the old river' E, which joined the Mole some 1400 metres downstream at F. This was successful as Raby states that 'we were never after flooded'. This implies that the work was done some years before Raby left Downside Mill in 1806 and it seems probable that it dates from the time when he was the tenant of Cobham Park in 1800.[15] This would also be consistent with additional work being needed following the severe floods of 1799 which destroyed one of the buildings at Cobham Mill. Watercourse E was later called 'the mill race' and a waterwheel by Whitmore & Binyon of Wickham Market, Suffolk, was installed on it in 1858.[16] It pumped water to Cobham Park and its location is indicated on figures 1 and 4.

Comparing the watercourses on Raby's plan of the mills, shown in figure 2, with those described in his letter, which cover the much larger area portrayed in figure 4, it is clear that the plan was prepared before the straight cut was dug across the 100 acres field. The approximate locations of the southern end of this cut and of the resulting narrower forge and tilt race 8 are shown by broken lines in figure 2. Clearly the former river channel between these watercourses had to be filled and confirmation of this is provided by a description of Cobham parish boundaries in 1815.[17] Starting at Ashford, B in figure 4, and moving southwards, the deviation G of the boundary from the river is described. This is probably related to waterworks associated with the former Ashford Mill or perhaps even to Raby's levelling of the river described in his letter. The boundary then follows the river to the point D where it is joined by the new cut and where Raby's dam had been made across the former channel. This abandoned channel is then followed to H 'the point of the iron mill premises where the stream divides'. The left-hand stream is then followed to I, 'the spot where the stream formerly ran which is now filled up, just at the sluices of the mills'. The sluices correspond to the forge and tilt race marked 8 on figure 2. The boundary then continues along the filled-up stream until it joins and crosses the new cut at J and continues to A.

Returning to the problem of dating the Raby plan, it has been suggested above that building the dam at D might well have occurred in about 1800 and it is possible that the new cut, which is not on the plan, was excavated shortly before this. Therefore the suggested date of about 1798 for the plan[18] is not unreasonable. This would have given Raby 28 years to rebuild and extend the mill buildings, resulting in rather complex shapes in many cases. It also means that a row of three cottages, which today stand on the site between buildings 23 and 32 of figure 2 but are not shown on the Raby plan, could be late eighteenth century, which appears to be the case.[19] If the 'women's shop' was associated with tinning in 1798 it indicates that this work was being carried out at least five years before Tinmans Row was built in 1803 but this is not unreasonable. Finally the paper on which the plan is drawn could have been stored in the surveyor's office for five or more years before it was used.

The sale by Raby of Downside Mill to John Bunn in 1806 adds little to our understanding of the work of the mill but the advertisement for the sale of the mill in 1809[20] is more helpful. It gives the head of water as 11 feet, states that there were two large anchorsmith's shops and mentions the coke oven. However it seems that it was anticipated that a new industry might be established at the site as it is stated that it was suitable for gunpowder, oil and paper manufacture as well as iron and copper working, wire making and corn milling.

After Alexander Raby

A summary of the main events associated with Downside Mill after Alexander Raby and John Bunn departed is given in table 3.

In 1810 the property was owned by Jackson & Co but in 1814 the iron mill was said to be dismantled.[21] Then in 1818 is was sold by John Hunter, William Bell and John Jackson.[22] The purchaser was Thomas Mellor, a horse hair manufacturer, and he established a flock mill on the site, at which old woollen cloth was cleaned and macerated to produce padding for mattresses and furniture. In 1839 seven men, one woman and eleven youths and boys worked at the mill and there was one waterwheel generating 30 hp.[23] This must have replaced the three waterwheels of building 13–18 in figure 2 and building 22–23 was probably no longer in use. Certainly this was the case in 1865 when the mill was again offered for sale. The particulars[24] state that there was a breast-shot waterwheel generating 36 hp and the accompanying plan shows that 22–23 had been replaced by a garden. The plan also shows a building on the site of the coke house, 25 of figure 2. This is not labelled, but it seems likely that it is the building described in the particulars as a drying house, where the used woollen cloth would have been dried after being washed and before being converted into flock. This building survives and has an unusual large-diameter chimney projecting from its roof. It is considered that this is associated with the drying house and has nothing to do with coke manufacture. By 1871 the premises had become a saw mill but 20 years later this was no longer working. In the 1890s a small waterwheel which generated electricity for Cobham Park was installed adjacent to the large waterwheel of building 13–18. Subsequently this building was used for storage but in the 1990s it was converted into offices, the remains of the waterwheels being retained and conserved.

Table 3. Brief chronology of Downside Mill after its occupation by Alexander Raby

1810	Owned by Jackson & Co
1814	Iron mill had been dismantled
1818	Sold by John Hunter, Wm Bell & John Jackson to Thomas Mellor
1818	Mellor establishes a flock mill at Downside
1839	7 men, 1 woman, 11 youths and boys, 30 hp waterwheel
1865	Downside flock mills for sale; 36 hp waterwheel
1871	'Downside Saw Mill' on 1:2500 OS map
1891	Saw mill no longer working
1890s	Small waterwheel generates electricity for Cobham Park
1925?	Mill closed and used for storage
1990s	Mill converted into offices; remains of waterwheel conserved

Appendix: Estimate of waterpower available at Downside Mill in late summer

At Molesey, in late summer, the typical flow of water along the River Mole is 45 cubic feet per second.[25] It is therefore estimated that the flow at Downside Mill, about 14 miles along the river upstream from Molesey, is about 40 cubic feet per second. The density of water is 62.5 lbs per cubic foot giving 2,500 lbs per second at Downside Mill, where the available head of water is about 11 ft. The approximate power available at Downside Mill is therefore 27,500 ft lbs per second which, as one horse power is 550 ft lbs per second gives about 50 hp. Frictional losses would reduce this to perhaps 30 hp. However 200 years ago there would have been more water in the river as there was less extraction, so rather more than 30 hp would have been available. This estimate matches the figures quoted in sale particulars of Downside Mill during the nineteenth century. Incidentally it takes about 5 hp to power one pair of corn millstones. Clearly in wetter seasons there would be more water but late summer flows are what determines the design of mill machinery. There was 50 times as much water flowing at Molesey during the flood of September 1968.

Notes and References

1. Walker, T E C, 'Cobham: manorial history', *Surrey Archaeological Collections,*, **58** (1961), 47–78, at 52–3, 60–2.
2. Crocker, A G, 'The paper mills of Surrey, part III', *Surrey History*, **5.1** (1994), 2–23, at 2–4.
3. Balston, J N, *The elder James Whatman, England's greatest paper maker (1702–1759)*, 2 vols (West Farleigh, the author, 1992), **1,** 285.
4. Shorter, A H, *Paper mills and paper makers in England 1495–1800*, (Hilversum, Paper Publications Society, 1957), 236.
5. Dagnall, H, *The taxation of paper in Great Britain, 1643–1861*, (Edgware, the author, 1998), 38–40.
6. Potter, J, 'Iron working in the vicinity of Weybridge, Surrey', *Industrial Archaeology Review*, **6.3** (Autumn 1982), 211–23, at 218.
7. Rees, A, *Rees's Manufacturing Industry (1819–20)*, ed. N Cossons, (5 vols, David & Charles Reprints, 1972), **3,** 187–91, 196–7, 202.
8. See Taylor, this volume, page 18.
9. Jenkins, R, *The collected papers of Rhys Jenkins*, (Newcomen Soc, 1936), 229.
10. See Taylor, this volume, pages 15–16.
11. *Ibid.*
12. Stidder, D, *The watermills of Surrey*, (Buckingham, Barracuda, 1990), 122.
13. Taylor, D C, *Cobham Characters* (Cobham, Appleton, 1998), 15–6; Stidder, ref. 12, 111.
14. SHC, Cobham land tax.
15. See Taylor, this volume, page 15.
16. Crocker, G, (ed), *A Guide to the industrial archaeology of Surrey*, (Association for Industrial Archaeology, 1990), 11.
17. Cobham parish church, vestry minute book.
18. Potter, ref. 6.
19. K Gravett, pers comm.
20. See Taylor, this volume, page 20.
21. Walker, ref. 1, 63.
22. See Taylor, this volume, page 20.
23. Greenwood, G B, *The Elmbridge water mills, Surrey*, (unpublished typescript, 1980).
24. D Taylor, pers comm.
25. Fish H, Harris B J D, Mander R J, Nicolson N J & Owen M, 'Rivers and Water', in *The Surrey Countryside*, ed. J E Salmon (University of Surrey for the British Association, 1975), 33–7.

Raby's Mill at Addlestone

DAVID BARKER

The construction and utilisation of a mill by Alexander Raby at Coxes Lock[1] on the Wey Navigation is well documented in the surviving archives of the Navigation. A detail of a 1782 plan of the Navigation, showing the site of the mill, is reproduced as figure 1. Raby's dealings with the waterway's owners, as well as his commercial links with the contemporary iron trade, are revealed in the Navigation archives. The development of the mill, although never as complex as some of his other activities, nevertheless illustrates a relatively well-recorded water-powered forge built for a specific operation and enhancing Raby's claim to be recognised as a major figure in the inter-related complexities of the eighteenth-century iron trade.

Prior to Raby's arrival at Addlestone, there appears to have been no mill adjacent to Coxes Lock. The first known documentary reference to the lock which gave its name to the site occurs in 1700 when £33 15s 10d was paid for scouring and fitting 'Cox Lock'.[2] In 1775 the lock, number 10, was surveyed by the owners, at which point it was noted that a tumbling bay would be useful near this lock.[3] The circumstances of Raby's involvement with his later works here are a little obscure. In July 1776, there were loaded at Godalming Wharf twenty ends of 6-inch-square oak timber totalling 466 feet, consigned to Raby & Co.[4] Although it is entirely possible that this substantial load of considerable dimensions was for another purpose, it is reasonable to suggest that it was to be used in the construction of the new mill.

The first mention of Raby in connection with the Mill building here occurs in 1777, when case papers referring to the new mills at Coxes Lock were prepared for the Navigation's proprietors and the following statement was recorded: 'Engineers have surveyed the spot and considered the whole scheme and are under certain directions in favour of it.' The record refers to 'making cuts or channels through the western banks of the river' (i.e. the Wey Navigation) 'to turn several wheels belonging to the mills they have erected'.[5] The extensive surviving records of the Navigation reveal much detail of the operation of the new mill. Coxes Lock is first mentioned as an unloading point when riverage was

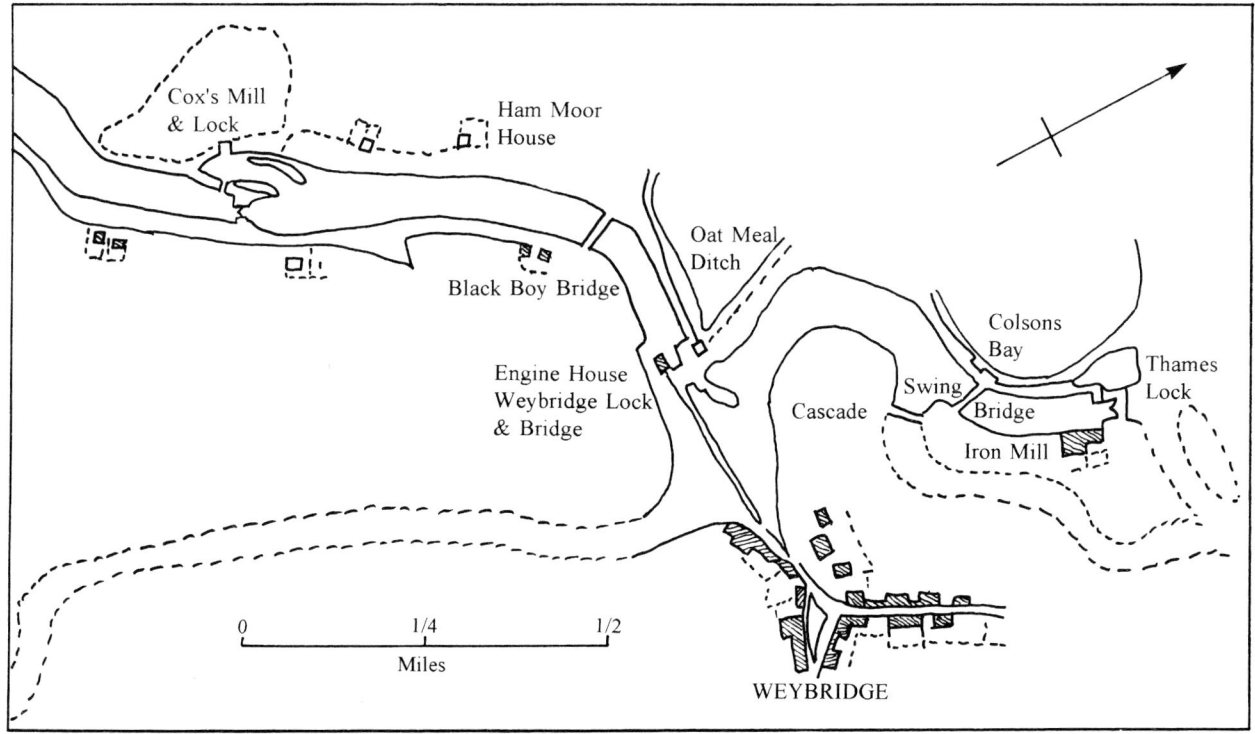

Figure 1. Redrawn detail of *A Plan of the River Wey, 1782*. (Surrey History Centre: G129/143/13).

charged to various barge proprietors for the quarter ending 31 December 1776.[6]

These initial references to Raby are replaced by references to Raby and Rodgers. Obadiah Wix Rodgers was an iron merchant in London and was presumably in partnership with Raby for the purpose of establishing the new venture at Addlestone. In fact, the new mill site was not an isolated one, because there had already been an iron hoop mill operating at Thames Lock (figure 1) on the same Navigation since 1720.[7] Moreover, metalworking was being carried out contemporaneously at the old-established mill site at Byfleet.[8] In view of his life-long connections with the iron trade in London and the Weald, Raby was no doubt fully aware of the potential of this new site. Its advantages were perhaps to be found in its position relatively near the Thames, while being at the same time geographically convenient to his other facility at Downside, Cobham, which appears to have been heavily developed by this time. There was also an existing local labour force well versed in the necessary skills for iron hoop production. Reputedly, £3000 was spent on the new venture, although the source of this information has not yet been confirmed. The advantages to the Navigation's owners were no doubt clear to them: the size of Raby's operation would soon generate significant revenues from tolls and rent. For instance, by 31 December 1777, $371\frac{1}{2}$ loads at one shilling per load had been carried to the site; and although the volumes fluctuated, it is clear that considerable revenue accrued to the owners of the waters.[9]

The background to the establishment of the new works must surely include reference to the historical situation of the time. Britain had commenced its conflict with the rebellious colonies in North America in 1776 and the Raby family had long experience of working with government departments and with private and mercantile traders in times of both war and peace. It must be assumed that government requirements alone would have necessitated increased demands for the product of a number of these north Surrey mills, i.e. barrel hoops. Also it seems useful to note the statements recorded by Weale concerning the supply of these hoops and the later establishment of Henry Cort's puddled and rolled iron processes.[10] Weale writes that 'the Victualling Board, in making their public contracts for that article, could procure supplies only from the different proprietors of mills in the vicinity of London, who combined together, at the time of tendering for the contracts, and of course, obtained the prices which they chose to demand, a certain proportion of the whole quantity required being allotted to each proprietor according to their private agreement; and that the Board, having no other recourse, could not remedy the above'. It is not unreasonable to assume that Raby was one of the very suppliers mentioned here: his later business dealings certainly suggest that he was quite capable of entering into such a cartel. Indeed, so critically important seems to have been the supply of these articles that, even with Raby's other facilities and his new Addlestone works, there came a time when it would appear that he was unable to supply iron hoops and is recorded as shipping wooden hoops from the Godalming area via the Navigation.[11]

In July 1782, Raby and Rodgers came to an agreement with the canal owners to cut channels through the west bank to build a tumbling bay and use the surplus water for turning the mill's wheels.[12] This contract also confirmed the use of the Navigation's water for an annual rental of £130 plus the payment of one shilling for every ton of iron or chaldron of coal carried from the Thames to the tail of the mill.[13] Here we have, for the first time, reference to the materials being carried to the site, although their use was implicit from its earliest operations. The agreement, for 16 years, was the forerunner of later agreements for the lease of the canal waters for the use of the mill for renewable periods of 21 years, thus also indicating the start of the Raby period in 1777. The character of Raby's dealings with the Navigation's owners is suggested in various references to disputes between the two parties over the operating of the facility here. In 1782 the canal owners were paying their agent to consult legal opinion in London as to what steps could be taken to prevent Coxes Mill from working.[14] All the while the facility was being operated and fees paid to the proprietors, further legal cases were being prepared against the offending operators and further expenses were incurred by the proprietors in seeking to have Raby tried for his misdemeanours in respect of the operating of the mill. However, the agreement of 25 July 1782 between Lord Milsinton and Bennett Langton – the proprietors of the canal – and Raby and Rodgers specifically forbade any business which made use of a great hammer.

The situation for Raby and, indeed, the country was, however, to change dramatically in the following year, when the peace brought about by the end of the American War of Independence had far-reaching implications for the iron trade in general. In January 1783, Alexander Raby wrote to the Navigation's proprietors in the following terms:

Sir – Having an opportunity of building a corn mill below Coxes Lock on Ham Common and erecting some iron forges near New Haw Lock, I should be obliged to you to inform the proprietors thereof and to request their permission and to take as much water of the Navigation as may be sufficient for working the corn mill and iron forges. This will obviously be of service to the proprietors and if they approve of it, will wait on you with further particulars. I should be glad of an early answer, that in case there should be no difficulty, I might be prepared to carry my plans into execution.[15]

By 14 March 1783, Raby was again petitioning the proprietors in the following terms:

Sir – Having received your answer informing me 'tis not at present agreeable to Lord Milsinton and Mr. Langton to permit me to make any erections at New Haw or Weybridge, I beg you'll request their permission for me to erect a hammer at Coxes Lock on the same water we now use, which our present licence does not permit us to do. The nature of the iron hoop trade being very much altered on account of the Peace makes it necessary for me to take some additional method for employing the water.[16]

In 1782 we find the first large-scale diagram of the new mill site (figure 1) contained in a plan of the whole length of the Navigation.[17] This is of interest in showing the layout of the mill buildings adjacent to the waterway, but also reveals some additional detail of the adjacent lands and includes a representation of a feature in dotted outline. This, on the site of the present reservoir, differs from its current profile and may suggest that Raby's permission to build a tumbling bay or head was acted upon in that same year to create what became one of the predominant features of the site, namely the $7\frac{3}{4}$-acre mill pond.

The same year also provides us with details of an interesting connection between Raby and other members of the contemporary iron trade, when a bond of indemnity was produced between Mr William Holmer of Thames Street, London, Ironmonger, and Lord Milsinton, a like bond from Richard Crawshaw of Thames Street, London, Ironmaster, and a like bond from James Spyers of Cheapside, London, Jeweller.[18] Holmer was, in fact, to join Raby in another apparent partnership, using the mill's facilities, and is recorded as paying riverage with Raby from 29 September 1784.

Raby's intended acquisition of property referred to earlier was completed when in September 1783 he purchased, for a consideration of 50 guineas, land adjacent to Pyrford Lock, New Haw Lock and Coxes Lock, together with part of Ham Moor, close to Coxes Lock, from John Ord and John Tyton under a marriage settlement of Thomas Onslow: Alexander Raby is noted as being of Cobham.[19] This purchase again seems to demonstrate Raby's considerable acumen in his business affairs and enabled him effectively to block competitors from taking the water of the Navigation for their own use at these key points. The Navigation accounts of 1783 record a total of $1693\frac{1}{2}$ loads carried to the tail of the mill, indicating the scale of Raby's activities even in this apparently difficult year. Raby's somewhat tempestuous relationship with the proprietors continued when, in the following year, they were put to expense and inconvenience in London concerning Raby's reported 'alterations at Coxes, which occasioned a very expensive breach above the Mill'.[20]

Some indication of the organisation on site is hinted at in 1790, when, according to the Weybridge parish records, James Welch, 'Clerk to the Mills at Coxes belonging to A. Raby', was buried – Addlestone at the time being included in the parish of Chertsey. In the same year there occurs yet another dispute between Raby and the proprietors, when they complained of the operation of a hammer at the site. The mill was visited by their agent, who reported back with the delightful description of the hammer's workings, illustrated by a pencil sketch, which is reproduced in facsimile in figure 2.[21]

During the course of Raby's occupation of the mill site, a revolution had taken place in the production of wrought iron, in terms of both its quality and quantity. This was occasioned largely by the introduction of Henry Cort's rolling and puddling patents in 1783 and 1784.[22] Indeed, as we have seen, Raby and his co-operators may well have been instrumental in bringing about these new techniques. In 1798, Raby's lease was due for renewal and in the following year he proposed to build a new mill.[23] It is not clear what occasioned this decision, i.e. whether he intended to embrace the new technology, now widely adopted by the iron trade, or whether the proposed new works were an addition to the existing operations which utilised the traditional techniques for producing hoop iron.[24]

Although the works appear not to have been built, in 1800 Raby is reported as constructing a new lime kiln at Coxes Lock.[25] This was recorded as being within 20 feet of the side of the lock wall, dug into the slope of the lock bank. The Navigation's agent told Raby that the proprietors would

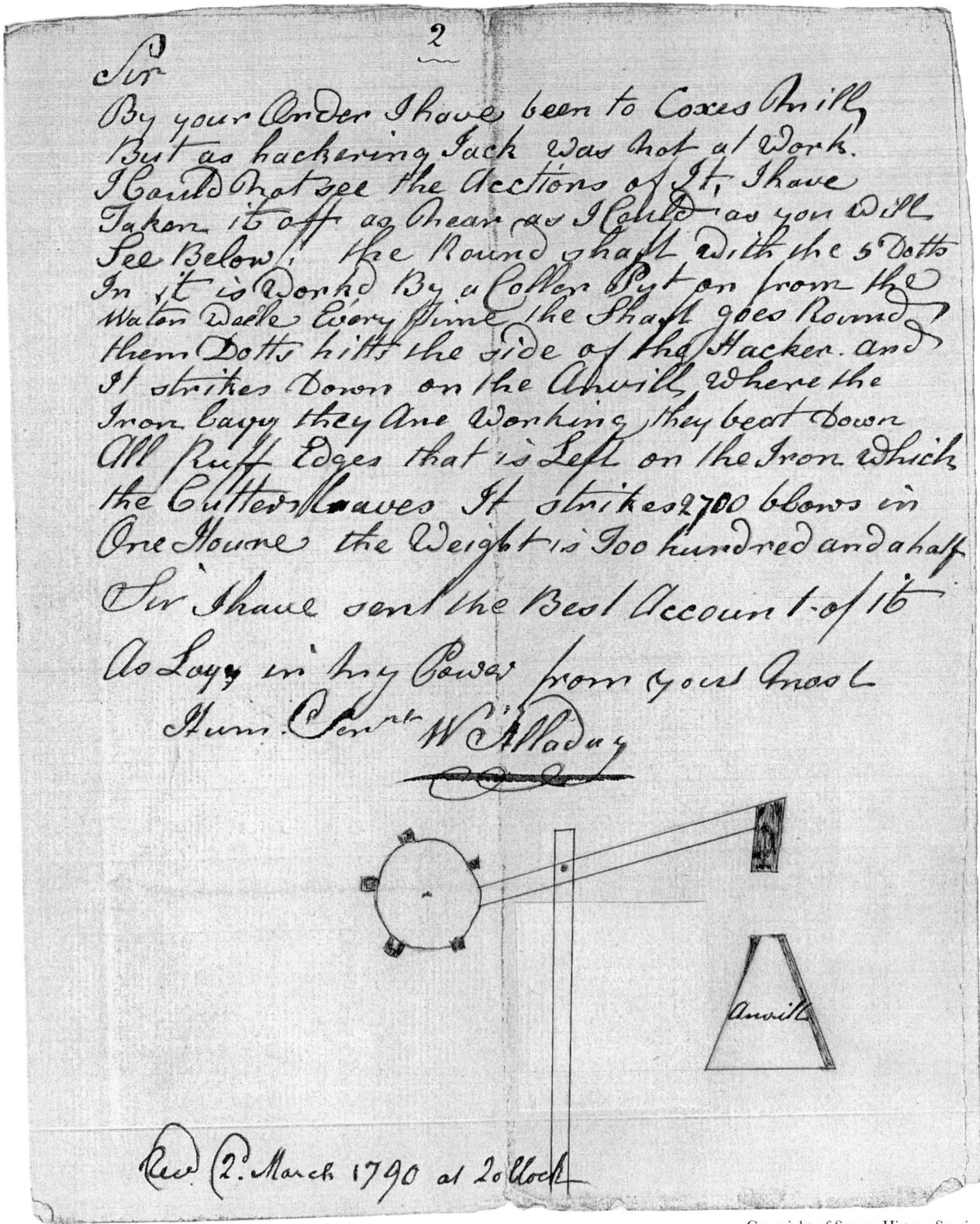

Figure 2. Description of Hackering Jack, the great hammer at Coxes Lock mill, 1790. Reproduced by permission of Surrey History Service (SHC: G129/42/2). The pencil sketch, which is faint in the original, has been retouched in this copy and an intrusive stamp has been removed. The text, also retouched, reads as follows:

Sir By your order I have been to Coxes Mill, but as hackering Jack was not at work I could not see the acctions of it. I have taken if off as near as I could as you will see below. The round shaft with the 5 dotts on it is worked by a coller put on from the water weele. Every time the shaft goes round them dotts hitts the side of the hacker and it strikes down on the anvill, where the iron lays they are working. They beat down all ruff edges that is left on the iron which the cutters leaves. It strikes 2700 blows in one houre. The weight is too hundred and a half. Sir I have sent the best account of it as lay in my power from your most humble Servant W. Alladay.

object, whereupon Raby replied that he had bought land within 14 feet of the lock and that he should do as he pleased. This single kiln may have been used for local building operations, though it may also have had a function as part of Raby's wider commercial interests, its convenience at Coxes being that a back cargo of chalk from the Guildford area may well have been a good commercial proposition for him, since he had fuel on site.

In 1799 the canal accounts produced the information that, during the quarter from 29 September to 31 December,1799, a total of 998 tons of iron, hoops, coal and gun carriages had been 'navigated' to and from Coxes Lock.[26] This again indicates the scale of the operations at the site at a time when, once again, the country was at war. The reference to gun carriages is intriguing: perhaps the site was producing cast gun carriages, or were they refurbishing or fitting ironwork on to the customary wooden constructions?

Raby's earlier purchase of land in the area of New Haw Lock seems to have entered into the equation of his complex operations because it is recorded that in 1804 'John Green and others with William Harrison at New Haw [were] setting out the land for the intended mill. John Sebthorpe, Guildford, [was] searching the Court Rolls to learn if Mr. Raby had purchased any land near New Haw Lock and he had'.[27] Although no structures ever appear to have been erected here for this purpose, the site of one of his properties immediately adjacent to the canal side at New Haw has revealed extensive dumping of iron slag and cinder, presumably from his works at Addlestone.[28] There is, however, an intriguing reference to a possible metal-working site at New Haw. Dr Sherlock, the Chertsey antiquarian, informed the author that he believed there was a foundry at New Haw, Addlestone, 'where a lime kiln now stands', two miles from Chertsey, though he could give no proof of his statement.[29] The plan of the site prepared for new owners in 1834, which shows the mill as a corn and silk mill (figure 3), clearly shows an area of open ground at present situated to the north of the mill buildings as occupied by Mr Raby's foundry.[30] However, there is little other evidence to suggest that the Coxes Lock site was utilised for casting operations. The 1794 *British Directory* entry for the area calls it 'Chertsey Mill, for forging and making iron hoops and bars'.

Though Coxes mill continued operating as a metal-working site until 1831, some indication of the condition of the works is revealed in a letter to the proprietors of the Navigation from the tenants who succeeded Raby.[31] This letter, dated 24 March 1810, refers to the 'very ruinous state of the mill and the use of fire engines[32] in iron manufactories in or near London and to the easy communication

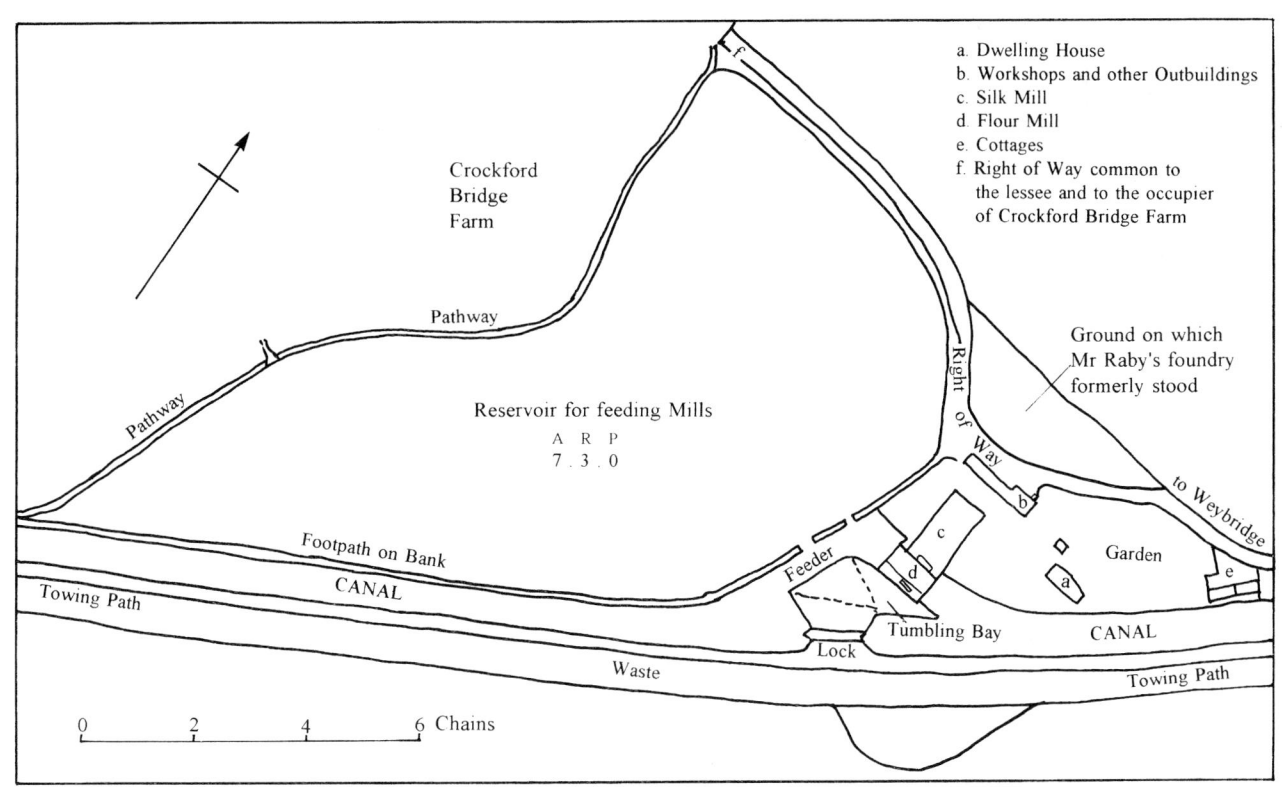

Figure 3. Redrawn map from a lease of 1834: Daniel Lambert of Brixton Hill, Esq. to Thos. W. Wood of Phipps Bridge Mills, Mitcham, silk throwster. (Surrey History Centre, G6/2/68).

now by canals from the country' and observes that 'the water situations are become of considerably less importance for the manufacture of iron'. The Thompson and Forman partnership had the licence to use the Navigation water assigned to them by Alexander Raby, it having been renewed in June 1798 for a further period of 21 years.

Raby's association with his mill site had ceased with his conveyance dated 3 January 1807 to John Taylor, an iron merchant of All Hallows, London, of the parcel of land originally purchased in 1783.[33] The mill and other ancillary buildings were still held by the original freeholder, Wilmot Lambert. Alexander Raby, by this time a resident of Llanelli, was busy consolidating his new enterprises in South Wales.

Thus ended Alexander Raby's control of his Addlestone mill. Its later development and subsequent growth into a major flour-milling centre remain to be committed to print. The structure as rebuilt for Thomas Wood (figure 3) continued to function until the 1980s, together with a new mill built in 1901 and a grain silo erected in 1904. This complex of listed buildings has subsequently been modified for residential use. Raby is however commemorated at the site he founded, where his name has been given to the block of luxury flats converted from the 1834 corn and silk mill.

Acknowledgements

I should like to thank the following for their help in the preparation of this paper: Mrs Pat Brown, without whose invaluable practical help it would not have been written, Alan Crocker for drawing the maps, the staff of the various Surrey Record Offices over many years, members of the Addlestone Historical Society and my wife Jocelyn for her forbearance during my continuing Raby researches.

Notes and references

1. Coxes is the present and recent form of spelling. Hearth Tax references for Chertsey parish refer to members of the Cock family and Jane Cocke claimed for damages in the Wey Navigation Claims (PRO: E177/1/85). Possibly the name is eponymous; later forms include Cox's and Coxe's. It was noted in discussion that there is no connection with Alexander Raby's wife, Mary Cox.
2. Surrey History Centre (SHC): G129/63/18.
3. SHC: G129/74a.
4. SHC: G142/2/1.
5. SHC: G129/39/12.
6. SHC: G129/29/4a.
7. SHC: G129/79/1.
8. Potter, J F, 'Iron Working in the Vicinity of Weybridge', *Industrial Archaeology Review*, **6** (Autumn 1982), 211–23.
9. The neighbouring iron works at the mouth of the Wey operated by Jukes Coulson were, however, paying a fixed fee of £30 per annum to the proprietors.
10. Science Museum Library, London, Weale MS, **1,** 76–79.
11. SHC: G142/2/1.
12. SHC: G129/10/41.
13. SHC: G129/10/41.
14. SHC: G129/7/4a.
15. SHC: G129/21/69. There is no evidence that a corn mill was actually built or operated at Coxes Lock before 1834/5.
16. SHC: G129/21/72.
17. SHC: G129/143/13.
18. SHC: G129/52/17.
19. SHC: 181/10/11.
20. SHC: G129/7/4a.
21. SHC: G129/42.
22. Pat. No. 1351 of 1783 relating to Preparing, Welding and Working Iron. Pat. No. 1420 of 1784 relating to the Manufacture of Iron.
23. SHC: G129/29/10.
24. SHC: G129/25/19 refers to a plan of the intended mill at Coxes Lock found on a list of the Wey Navigation's archives drawn up in 1830. Alas, the document was not found when the collection was catalogued in 1967.
25. SHC: G129/29/58.
26. SHC: G129/22/106.
27. SHC: G129/104/1.
28. Thanks are due to Mr and Mrs Payne of New Haw for drawing attention to these dumps.
29. Stahlschmidt, J C L, *Surrey Bells Founders*, (London, 1884), 112.
30. SHC: G6/2/68.
31. SHC: G129/69/1.
32. The term fire engine was used for steam engine.
33. SHC: G129/6/2/15.

Alexander Raby – Ironmaster and Coalmaster

LYN JOHN

The eighteenth century saw the start of the Industrial Revolution which caused major changes to the skills, environment and working conditions of the people of Great Britain. The town of Llanelli's own industrial revolution started when an Englishman crossed the town's Falcon Bridge with a train of wagons carrying his family, his possessions and a large chest of gold.[1] He was to be the catalyst that transformed the town from a small fishing village of 56 houses and a parish church into one of the major coal and steel towns of South Wales. Alexander Raby, 'tall, handsome, high-minded, eccentric, always doing strange acts of kindness'. These are a few of the words used to describe the man by past historians.[2] He was also an entrepreneur, ironmaster and coal baron who came to Llanelli around 1796 to gamble his entire fortune in the coal and iron industries but left in reduced circumstances.

Alexander Raby's first connection with the town is said to have begun when he financed John Gevers and Thomas Ingman, two iron-founders who had previously set up an iron furnace on the Stradey Estate in 1791.[3] Little is known about these men, except that they leased some farms locally where there were sources of ironstone.[4] According to early historians, Gevers and Ingman were not successful and were unable to repay Raby who then foreclosed on them and took over the iron furnace in 1796. John Gevers continued to work with Raby at the Stradey furnace and was to be associated with him for many years. Raby had business interests in other parts of Wales including Cilgerran, Neath, Swansea, Morriston, Saundersfoot and in England at Cobham.[5] The great revolution in iron making meant that good quality iron could now be made with coal in the form of coke. For economic and logistical reasons it was necessary for iron manufacture to be sited near the source of its raw materials. Coal was king!

The town of Llanelli was already known for its trade in coal. It was probably for this reason that Raby relocated there from Cobham. He worked a number of coal mines on the Stradey Estate, including pits called Caerelms, Caemain and Caebad. Indeed, it was on the Stradey Estate that he centred his industrial operations. The estate was owned during Raby's time by Dame Mary Anne Mansel, who bequeathed it to Thomas Lewis on her death in 1808. Raby's relationship with both these landowners can be described as being, at the least, stormy.

As well as building a second furnace at Stradey in 1800, Raby built his home there, in a valley called Cwmddyche, which has been translated as 'pleasant valley' or 'useful valley'. The village itself became known as Furnace, as marked on the map in figure 1. This shows the district, and the principal sites associated with the Raby family, in 1878. Alexander Raby's house, named *The Dell* on the map, was originally called 'Furnace House'. Both his sons, Alexander junior and Arthur, lived close by, Alexander junior at *Bryn-mor* and Arthur at 'Plas Ucha', which was on the site of *Cae-mawr Cottage* on the map. One furnace, marked *Old Furnace* on the map, is still extant and was made a Listed building in 1966 but little has been done to preserve it. A sketch of the surviving structure is shown in figure 2.

After taking over the ironworks in 1796, Raby pushed them to their maximum output during the French wars, producing armaments for the war effort. A contemporary newspaper, *The Cambrian*, reports in February 1804: 'So prompt are the measures of government at this time, that four furnaces of different description are at work night and day at Llanelly, solely confined to the service of the Board of Ordnance'. Raby & Company (Carmarthenshire) were frequent contractors to the Board. Payments to the company for carronades and round shot have been noted in the Board's records and evidence has also been found of Raby carronades being carried by warships at Chatham Dockyard.[6] Carronades were short, light guns nicknamed 'smashers' because they fired heavy shot at close range. They took their name from the Carron Iron Works in Scotland where they were first made. Raby's guns were marked on the trunnions with the letters R or AR.[7] *The Cambrian* also reports that one shipment of ordnance sent from Llanelli to London, on board the vessel *The Mary Anne*, was captured off Beachy Head by a French privateer in 1804.

It is evident that at the beginning of nineteenth century Raby's empire was expanding. By 1804 he had constructed a new forge where pig iron was

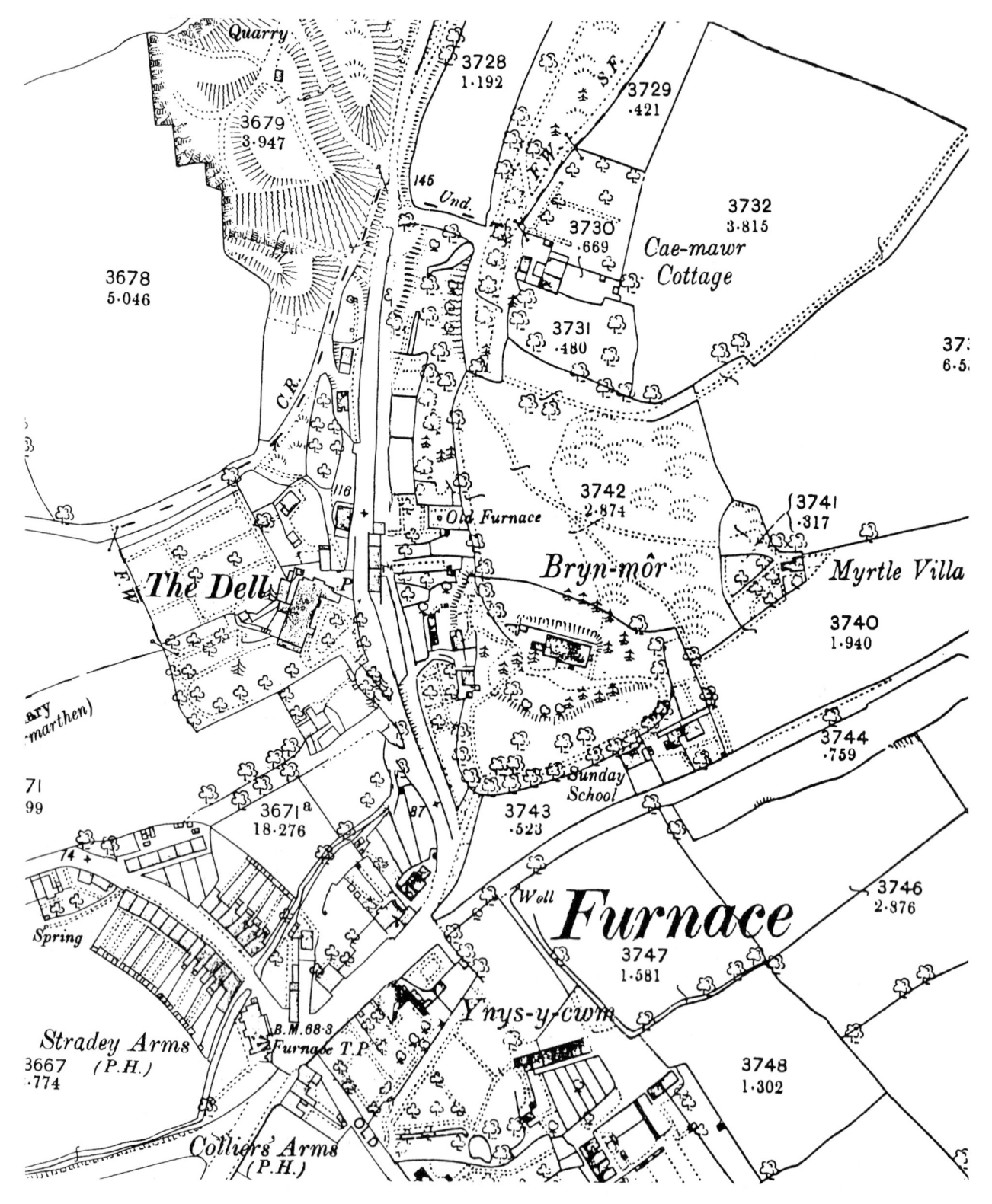

Figure 1. The village of Furnace, Llanelli, from the Ordnance Survey 25-inch map surveyed 1878. Sites associated with the Raby family are as follows: The Dell or Furnace House *(Alexander Raby's house)*, Cae-mawr Cottage *(the site of Arthur Raby's house, 'Plas Ucha')*, Bryn-mor *(Alexander Raby junior's house)*, Ynys-y-cwm *(the railway office and weigh bridge, sometimes called 'Machine House')*. The Carmarthenshire Railroad followed the line of the road running roughly north-eastwards past the Collier's Arms and Ynys-y-Cwm and to the south of Bryn-Mor. The furnace pond occupied the plot numbered 3728 on the east side of the quarry to the north. Its outlet can be followed south towards Old Furnace, the remains of which are shown in figure 2. The legend Furnace T.P, near the road junction by the Colliers' Arms, marks a toll gate on the Furnace turnpike.

Figure 2. Alexander Raby's furnace. Drawing by Neville Tonge.

converted into wrought iron and rolled into bars, rods and rails. He constructed a dock, once known locally as Squire Raby's Dock. He embraced new technology for, in that same year, he installed one of Trevithick's new high-pressure steam engines at Caebad colliery. His furnaces and forge were also powered by steam. Through his agents James Goodyear, George Walker and Robert Parkin, Raby owned four ships.[8] He set up an artery of tramways linking all his sites from his furnaces down to his dock. The small town of Llanelli experienced a population explosion, growing from under 500 inhabitants in 1795 to just under 3000 by 1801. To meet the demand for housing Raby built over a hundred cottages.[9] Some were sited near his collieries and furnaces but the biggest housing development was *Forge Row*, 34 cottages next to his forge which were demolished in the early 1930s. At the end of this row stood a public house appropriately called the *Raby Arms*.[10]

Iron production required large quantities of coal, limestone and iron ore. Coal was obtained locally from collieries on the Stradey estate and was initially transported by mules and oxen, but Raby had to go further afield to obtain the limestone and iron ore. There were quarries for both on Mynydd Mawr (Great Mountain) 13 miles north of Llanelli. An economic method of transportation was essential to move the large quantities required for the furnaces. Although a canal was initially considered, it was finally decided that a railway or tramway would be most efficient[11] and, as the enormous expense would have been prohibitive to Raby himself, it was decided to fund it by public subscription. A petition was presented to the House of Commons for a railway or tramroad to be constructed from Llanelli to Mynydd Mawr and an Act of Parliament was passed on 3 June 1802 allowing its construction.[12] Its route followed the line of the road which runs roughly WSW–ENE across the map in figure 1. Its motive power was horse power – although the stationary steam engine was in use, it would be another two years before Richard Trevithick's famous steam locomotive was to run on the Penydarren Tramroad at Merthyr Tydfil.

Raby had everything to gain. Not only would he sell his existing tramway linking his dock and his furnaces to the newly formed Carmarthenshire Rail Road Company, but also the potential local demand for cast-iron rails, plates and wheels would provide a ready market for the iron from his furnaces. Raby sold his section of railway to the company for £3117.[13] This section became the oldest public railway in use in Great Britain.[14]

Business was booming. Raby's workers were well paid – so well paid that they were said to 'eat pound notes on well buttered sandwiches'! Alexander Raby was well-liked by the town's populace. Who was this Englishman who initiated the town of Llanelli's industrial revolution? Arthur Mee paints him as a kind and benevolent character, quoting a number of his charitable deeds. He once met a travelling pack-boy and was so impressed by the boy's sharpness that he gave him a job as a clerk in his counting house. While visiting Carmarthen Jail on business he became acquainted with a gentleman who was locked up for debt and was, once again, so impressed by the man's conversation that he obtained his release by paying off the debt and giving the man a clerkship. While visiting London he met an old friend and employee who had fallen on hard times; Raby brought him back to Wales and put the man up in his own home, employing him as his confidential agent.[15] Samuel Smiles states that Raby was 'the best authority on the iron trade in the last [eighteenth] century'.[16] The Raby family were part of the Llanelli gentry, attending many a social function at the town's Falcon Hotel. Alexander and his sons, Alexander junior and Arthur, were involved in the early administration of the town as they were town burgesses and active members of the Harbour Trust.[17] In 1809 Raby's eldest son, Alexander junior, married Jane Rees, daughter of the local squire John Rees of Cilymaenllwyd,[18] and in 1813 Arthur married Henrietta Jane Smith, whose family is said to have owned estates in the West Indies.[19]

Although Raby's empire appeared to be flourishing, storm clouds were gathering, for by 1806 the shareholders of the Carmarthenshire Rail Road Company were not receiving the expected returns on their investments. Alexander Raby faced a financial crisis from which he never fully recovered. He had misused the assets of the railway company. In effect, he had installed unauthorised tramways and railways at his furnaces, forge and collieries and, to make matters worse, had avoided the payment of tolls to the company. All these criticisms were included in a damning report to the company in August 1806.[20] At the same time, Thomas Lewis of Stradey was pursuing Raby for £1000, for non-payment of rents on the Stradey estate. By June 1807 Raby was forced to convene a meeting of his creditors at which he had to assign to them his principal estates, including some of his properties in London and Cobham, although he was allowed to retain control of his works. However, he was given some respite from this crisis as he had developed the Box Colliery, which boasted a 9-foot seam of coal.[21]

Financial problems continued to plague him and by 1809 he was once again in serious financial difficulty. In October and November of that year his entire iron works and collieries at Llanelli and Neath were advertised for sale in *The Cambrian*. The sale was to take place by auction at Garraway's Coffee House, London, on 16 November. It was at about this time that Raby was forced to sever connection with his industry at Cobham. Although his failure is generally attributed to his misuse of the Carmarthenshire Railway assets, the onset of his financial problems appears to have occurred in 1803.[22] It was then that he dissolved a partnership with a certain Colonel John Dumaresq, who owned a quarter share in the works and collieries in Llanelli. Raby had, in effect, bought Dumaresq out, on a long-term basis, by paying him fixed amounts with interest. Following the Carmarthenshire Railway enquiry in 1807, Raby's entire concern at Llanelli was put into the hands of trustees. These were Messrs Hammet, Thompson, Day, Handasyde & Birch, who took over management of the concern in 1808. Raby also faced considerable debts from his iron and coal concern at Neath in Glamorganshire, where he was pursued by Lord Vernon for arrears of rent in 1810.[23] By this time, Raby was insolvent. His trustees then took over management of the works, to their great loss,[24] and were probably responsible for the attempted sale at Garraway's Coffee House, which did not appear to materialise any buyers. By 1811 Raby's empire had become a 'hot potato'.

It appears that the trustees were a wealthy group of personal friends of Raby and were happy to sell the property back to him and his new partner, his son Arthur, now aged 21, hoping that he might obtain some income from it. As Raby was insolvent, he sought finance from another group of friends, Charles Druce and Richard Janion Nevill. The latter and his father Charles Nevill were proprietors of a large copper works to the south of Llanelli,- which they had erected in about 1805. Druce was a wealthy London attorney who had been a lifelong and 'zealous' friend of Alexander Raby. From time to time, Nevill and Druce provided financial support for the Rabys throughout their remaining years in business.[25]

Raby and son continued in partnership in their iron and coal concern, producing coal for both the home and export markets and manufacturing such items as tram wheels and iron naves for wheels for local collieries. Problems continued to befall the Rabys. Lack of orders for their iron works must have been the reason for the stoppage of the furnaces, which were said to have been blown out by 1815, the same year as the Battle of Waterloo and the end of the Napoleonic Wars.[26] The Rabys now sought assistance from Arthur Raby's brother-in-law, George Haynes, of Haynes, Day, Haynes & Lawrence, a Swansea bank. Along with Nevill and Druce, initially they must have seen the Raby empire as a potential investment for their monies for they continued to support both Alexander and Arthur for some time with the expectation of some returns on their loans. However, Richard Janion Nevill of the copper works had another motive. The copper works relied on the collieries of a certain General George Warde for their supply of coal. Had Raby gone under, the copper works would have been at the mercy of Warde who would then have had a monopoly of the coal market at Llanelli. Furthermore, had Raby's collieries closed, all his collieries would have sustained permanent damage by flooding, thus reducing any chance of recovering monies owed to the increasing number of creditors who were awaiting payment. The pumps had to be kept going![27]

By 1820 the Rabys were in debt to Nevill and Druce in sums exceeding £10,000 To help pay off these debts the Rabys agreed to supply coal to the copper works at reduced rates. The next five years proved to be the end of the Raby empire. The year 1820 also saw the stoppage of the forge.[28] All that now remained to support the Rabys were the leases that they held on their collieries at Llanelli and the coal sales from these mines. By now they were termed 'coalmasters'. At the age of 76, Alexander senior decided to retire and on 1 December 1823 consigned the concern to his son Arthur, who continued to be financed by his brother-in-law George Haynes of the Haynes Bank. The following year saw the death of Alexander's wife Ann aged 78. Her grave can still be seen today at Llanelli Parish Church. This sad loss to Alexander may have prompted him to make his will, in which he consigned all to his son Arthur, subject to his paying allowances to his brother and cousin. That same year, 1824, saw the destruction of Arthur's house by fire. The house, roofed with thatch, was totally consumed in a short time.[29] This was not the only disaster to befall the family for the final nail in the coffin was a crisis of national importance. The economic markets of the banking world were thrown into confusion by over-speculation in new markets in South America. This crisis caused the failure of the Haynes Bank of Swansea, which in turn caused the ultimate failure of the Raby empire in 1825.[30]

Raby and his son, now owing very large sums of money to Nevill, Druce, Messrs Haynes and an extraordinary number of workmen, tradesmen and shopkeepers, were forced to hand over their entire concern at Llanelli to Messrs Broom & Guthrie[31] who acted as trustees for Nevill and Druce. The Rabys were forced to leave the country and spent the next five years travelling to-and-fro between France and Jersey. They finally returned to England and settled at Burcott House near Wells in Somerset and Alexander was said to be 'seen now and then' in the streets of Bath. As he approached the age of 88, the pages closed on Alexander's busy life at Burcott on 24 February 1835.[32] His remains were laid to rest in St Cuthbert's Church, Wells.

The passage of time has made it difficult to pinpoint the actual cause or causes of the failure of Raby's industrial empire but historians have put forward various suggestions: the fact that there was an economic depression following the end of the war with France; that the distance from Raby's furnaces to his ironstone mines was too great; that the quality of the iron ore was poor, giving a poor yield (he had been importing ore from Lancashire and Anglesey). It could be that Raby had had put all his eggs into one basket. He had restricted his market to the production of tram plates for the Carmarthenshire Rail Road and the supply of armaments to the government, so that when both these markets dried up he had no customers. Recent research by Davies failed to reveal orders for cannon or shot for the Board of Ordnance later than 1805.[33] This may have been because the victory at Trafalgar meant that the threat of invasion was over and lessened the demand for ordnance.

Although Alexander Raby's business empire failed in Llanelli, he is credited by most historians as being the pioneer of the town's industrial development. By 1886 the once small fishing village had grown into one of the major industrial towns of South Wales, boasting seven large tinplate works, a large copper works, four large foundries, a lead and silver works, a ship-building yard, three steam-powered saw mills and half-a-dozen collieries which exported 87,500 tons of coal in that year.[34] Now all that remains in the town in connection with Alexander Raby is the ruin of his blast furnace and the name of the village, Furnace, in which it stands. Both are fitting memorials to this great industrialist.

Acknowledgements

Thanks are due to Dr M V Symons, Dr J D Davies, Peter Benians, David Taylor and John Edwards and to Richard Davies and the staff of Llanelli Public Library.

Notes and References

1. Innes, J, *Old Llanelly* (1904), 75.
2. Mee, A, *Llanelli Parish Church* (1888), ch.VI.
3. Bowen, D, *Hanes Llanelli* (1856, English translation).
4. Symons, M V, Coal Mining in the Llanelli Area (Llanelli Borough Council, 1979); Brian Cripps, postal historian, private collection: Gevers and Ingman letter.
5. Llanelli Public Library (LPL), LC 1572: Thomas Mainwaring Papers.
6. Dr David Davies, pers comm.
7. Kennard, A N, *Gunfounding and Gunfounders* (1986), 131.
8. *The Cambrian*, 24 Feb. 1804.
9. Mainwaring, ref. 5.
10. *Pigot's Directory*, 1844.
11. *Rees Cyclopedia* (1812), Canals, pp.353, 358.
12. 42 Geo III, cap 80, (3 June 1802).
13. Symons, ref. 4, 209. The company is sometimes referred to as the Carmarthenshire Railway Company.
14. Price, M R C, *The Llanelly and Mynydd Mawr Railway* (The Oakwood Press, 1992), 17; Cadw: Welsh Historic Monuments Executive Agency, Scheduling entry CAM 1/1/6616.
15. Mee, ref. 2, ch.VI.
16. Smiles, S, *Iron Workers and Toolmakers* (1897), 121.
17. LPL: Burgesses' Book; Harbour Commissioners' Book.
18. Burke's *History of the Commoners* vol. 3 (1836), 267.
19. *The Cambrian*, 16 Oct. 1813.
20. LPL, LC 257: Notes on the Llanelli furnace.
21. LPL, LC 575: Symons, M V, 'Box Colliery'.
22. LPL, Nevill Industrial Records: item 7.
23. Phillips, R, *A Romantic Valley in Wales – The History of the Vale of Neath* (1925), 305.
24. LPL, Nevill Industrial Records: Letter 442, 9/4/1838.
25. LPL, Nevill Industrial Records: Letter 458, 30/5/1838.
26. Innes, J, ref. 1, 105.
27. LPL, Nevill Industrial Records: Letter 557, 29/7/1839.
28. Innes, ref. 1, 105.
29. *The Cambrian*, 29 May 1824.
30. *Chronicle of Britain*, ed Henrietta Heald (Chronicle Communications Ltd, 1992), 837.
31. LPL, Nevill Industrial Records: Letter 497, 2/2/1839.
32. *Bath Chronicle*, 26 Feb. 1835.
33. Dr David Davies, pers comm.
34. Wilkins, C, *The South Wales Coal Trade and its Allied Industries* (1888), 42, 43.

Appendix

Summary of Raby entries in London trade directories, 1749–1811

PETER JENKINS

The Guildhall Library contains a nearly continuous collection of London trade directories from 1736. Examination of those for the period 1736 to 1815 gave the following locations, names and trades involving the Raby family and their associates. While the name Raby is unusual, caution needs to be taken in assuming that all the entries refer to the same person, eg those for G Raby, who may or may not be Alexander's nephew George. No entries for Alexander Raby were noted after 1811.

A. 1749–1765: In Smithfield as Master[1] & Raby, ironmongers

B. 1766–1775: No references in which Raby's name comes first.

C. 1776–84: In Mill Street, Dockhead, as Raby & Rogers, iron hoop manufacturers[2]

D. 1785–1805: On a site off Upper Thames Street running between the Steelyard and Allhallows Lane, Alexander Raby entered variously as a merchant, iron merchant and iron hoop manufacturer, either alone or with the following associates:
   William Holmer, as merchants or iron merchants, 1785–1797.[3]
   Obadiah Rogers, as iron hoop manufacturers, 1790.[4]
   George Raby, as merchants or iron merchants, 1792–1796.[5]

E. 1788–1804: Alexander Raby at 15 Bush Lane,[6] between Upper Thames Street and Cannon Street, as a merchant or iron merchant, alone or with:
   George Raby, 1792–1793.[7]

F. 1797–1798: At Cobham, near Guilford, as merchant.

G. Private addresses:
   Alexander Raby, Broad Sanctuary, Westminster, 1802 and 1811.
   Mr Raby, St. George's-row, New Houses, 1808.

Notes

1. Edward Raby and Alexander Master had been apprenticed to Ambrose Crowley and Alexander Raby was bound apprentice to Master in 1762. Alexander Master is referred to as an ironmonger in Smithfield 1738–1745 and Kent's Directory of 1765 and 1767 gives his address at Bayle's Apothecary, Smithfield. No later reference to Alexander Master was noted.
2. Rogers is called 'junior' in about half the references. While the name Rogers is frequently mentioned there is no reference to a Rogers senior in any iron trade.
3. William Holmer in mentioned as a merchant trading from this site, 1779–1784, and also as an ironmonger trading from 165 Borough High Street from 1765 to after 1815. Holmer, Dubuisson & Summerland also traded from this site, 1781–1784.
4. This is only in Wakefield's Directory and might be an error. Wakefield also mentions O W Rogers as an iron merchant at Dockhead in 1790 and 1794, but other directories of these years do not.
5. Possibly a nephew? George is also mentioned, as an ironmonger, 31 Greek Street, Soho, 1799–1808 and G Raby, as a broker, 33 Great St Helen, 1811. A George Raby was granted Patent No 1176 on 7 January 1778, 'Instrument, or a silver coin balance, for detecting base half-crowns, shillings or sixpences'.
6. Some references give the number as 27 Bush Lane but this could be a printer's error. The tax registers are no help as numbers are not given. Alexander Raby's livery is given as the Draper's Company in 1798.
7. As there is an overlap with item D, this could possibly have been his private residence. It exits into Upper Thames Street between Steelyard and Allhallows Lane. Other houses nearby were private residences.

Index of Persons, Places and Organisations

Abbreviations: f: founder; mf: manufacturer; pm: papermaker; pr: proprietor; Sx: Sussex; Sy: Surrey.

Abinger Hammer, Sy, 7
Abington, William, of Cobham, 17
Addlestone, Sy, 11, 29, 31
Alfieri, Count Vittorio, poet, 16
Alladay, W, agent, 32
Anglesey, 39
Ashford, Sy, 17, 26; Farm House, 16, 17; mill 15, 22, 26
Ashburnham furnace, Sx, 3

Barry, E M, architect, 16
Basted mill, Wrotham, Kent, 23
Bell, William, merchant, 20, 27
Bermondsey, 15
Berrey (Borroy), William, pm, 23
Bicknell, John, pm, 22, 23
Board of Ordnance, 2, 4, 5, 6, 7, 35, 39
Bowen, William, f, 6
Box Colliery, 38
Bray, Henry, miller, 25
Bristol, 3
Brooklands, Sy, iron age site, 9, 11
Broom & Guthrie, Messrs, trustees, 39
Bunn, John, iron merchant, 9, 18, 19, 20, 20n, 23, 27
Byfleet mill, Sy, 11, 12, 30

Caebad colliery, 35
Caemain colliery, 35
Caerelms colliery, 35
Carhampton, Henry Lawes Luttrell, Earl of, 16, 18
Carmarthenshire Rail Road Co., 38, 39
Carron Co., Falkirk, 6, 35
Carshalton mill, Sy, 23
Chertsey, Sy, 31, 33; abbey 22
Churchill, John, f, 3
Cilgerran, Cardiganshire, 35
Clutton, William, f, 5, 6
Cobham, Sy, 15, 17, 18, 19, 22, 35, 38, 41; mill 15, 26; Park (see also Downe Place), 13, 15, 17, 18, 19, 20, 26, 27; Park estate, 15
Cock(e) family, 34n
Coleridge, Samuel Taylor, 16
Combe, Harvey, of Cobham Park, 17, 18; Harvey Christian 18, 20, 20n
Cort, Henry, ironmaster, 30, 31
Coulson, Jukes, f, 34n
Cox, Ann, wife of Alex. Raby, 15
Coxes Lock, 29; mill 11, 12, 13, 15, 18, 29-34
Crawshaw, Richard, iron mf, 31
Crowley family, iron mfs, 1, 2, 3; Ambrose, 1; Sir Ambrose 1, 2; John 1
Cwmddyche, Llanelli, 35

Dale Abbey Ironworks, Derbs, iii
Darwell furnace, Sx, 3
Derwent valley, Co. Durham, 1
Down(e) Manor, Sy, 22, 23; Place (see also Cobham Park), 15-16, 16, 18, 22, 23
Downside (Down(e)) mill, Sy, 11, 12, 13, 15, 17, 18, 20, 22-8
Down, Thomas a, 22
Downside bridge, 13; common, 18
Drapers' Company, 1, 2, 41
Druce, Charles, attorney, 38-9
Dumaresq, Col. John, 38

East India Company, 4, 5, 6, 7
Ember mill, Sy, 12, 13; river, 11, 13
English & Bradley, Messrs, fs, 7
Esher mill, Sy, 11

Falkirk 6
Foley family, iron mfs, 1, 2
Forest of Dean, 1
France, 5, 39
Freeland, George, of Ashford, 18
Furnace, Llanelli, 18, 35, 36, 40

Garraway's Coffee House, 20, 38
Garton, John, of Downside mill, 23
Gevers, John, f, 35
Gloucester furnace, Lamberhurst, Kent, 7
Godalming, 11, 30; Navigation 11, 30; wharf 29
Goodyear, James, agent, 37
Gravetye furnace, Sx, 5, 6
Great Bookham, Sy, 22
Green, John, building surveyor, 33
Greenwich, 1
Guildford, Sy, 33
Gwilt, George, engineer, 18

Ham Common, 31; Moor 31; Ham Haw (Thames Lock) mill, 20n
Hamilton, Hon. Charles, of Painshill Park, 15
Hammet, Thompson, Day, Handasyde & Birch, Messrs, 7
Hanbury, Major John, 1
Harrison & Bagshaw, Messrs, fs, 7
Harrison, William, building surveyor, 33
Haynes, George, banker, 39
Haynes, Day, Haynes & Lawrence, Messrs, bankers, 39
Hillier (Hillyer) family, pms, 15, 22; John 23; Thomas 22, 23; Mary 22, 23
Hinton, Richard, pm, 22, 23
Holmer, William, ironmonger, 31, 41
Holmer, Dubuisson & Summerland, merchants, 41
Howbourne forge, Sx, 6
Hunt, Joseph, pm, 15, 23; Elizabeth 23
Hunter, John, merchant, 20, 27

India, 4
Ingman, Thomas, f, 35
'Ironworks in Partnership', 1

Jackson & Co, ironmongers, 18, 20, 27
Jersey, 39
Jukes, George and William, fs, 3

Knight, Richard, of Stour Partnership, 2
Knight, Robert, carrier, 3, 5, 6

Lambert, Wilmot, landowner, 34
Lancashire, 39
Lanesborough, Viscountess, of Down Place, 22
Langton, Bennett, canal pr, 30, 31
Lewis, Thomas, landowner, 35, 38
Ligonier, Field Marshall Lord John, 16, 20n; Edward, 2nd Earl, 16
Little Bookham, Sy, 22, 26
Llanelli, 15, 18, 34, 35-40; harbour trust, 38; parish church, 39

Lloyd, Francis, MP, 20n; Elizabeth (Graham), 20n
Lloyd, Sampson, ironmonger, 1
London, 1, 2, 11, 12, 15, 30, 38
Lucy, Thomas, miller, 21n, 26
Lucy's mill, Cobham, 18, 26
Lyfield, Thomas and Frances, landowners, 22

Macky, Robert, importer, 2, 5
Mansel, Dame Mary Anne, landowner, 35
Master, Alexander sr, ironmonger, 2; Alexander jr, 2, 3, 5, 6, 41; Mary, 2; Walter, 2
Master and Raby, Messrs, 2, 3, 4, 5, 7, 15, 41
Mee, Arthur, writer, 38
Meers, John, pm, 23
Mellor, Thomas, horsehair and flock mf, 20, 27
Mereton, Mr, banker, 11, 15
Merthyr Tydfil, 38
Milsinton, Lord, canal pr, 30, 31
Mole river, 11, 15, 17, 18-19, 22, 25-6, 27; valley, 9
Momma, Jacob, brass mf, 13
Monmouth canal, 17
Morris, Thomas, of Down mill, 22, 23
Morriston, Glamorgan, 35
Moss, William, of Cobham, 18

Neath, Glamorgan, 35, 38
Nevill, Charles and Richard Janion, copper mfs, 38-9
New Haw, Sy, 31, 33; lock 31
North America, 4, 5, 30
North Park furnace, Haslemere, Sy, 7

Old Swinford, Worcs, 1
Onslow, Thomas, landowner, 31
Ord, John, agent, 31

Page, Mr, of Cobham, 18
Painshill Park, Sy, 15
Parker, Thomas & Co., fs, of Bristol, 4
Parkin, Robert, agent, 37
Penydarren Tramroad, 37-8
Portmore, Lord, 12
Pyrford lock, Sy, 31

Raby, Alexander, *passim*; Alexander jr (1) 16, (2) 16, 35; Ann 39; Arthur 35, 39; Arthur Turnour 16; Catherine 16; Edward 1, 2, 5, 6, 7, 15, George, 41, Margaret Maria 16; Mary (Master) 15; William, 1; & Co. (Carmarthenshire), 35; and Master, 2, 3, 15; and Mereton, 15, 23; and Rogers, 12, 15, 30, 41
Rees, Jane, wife of Alex. Raby jr, 38; John, of Cilymaenllwyd, 38
Robertsbridge furnace and forge, Sx, 3
Rogers, Obadiah Wix, ironmaster, 7, 12, 15, 30, 41
Royal Arsenal, Woolwich, 4, 5, 7

St George's Hill, Weybridge, Sy, 9, 13
Saundersfoot, Pembroke, 35
Sebthorpe, John, attorney, 33
Sharp & Kirkup, Messrs, auctioneers, 20
Sherlock, Dr, antiquarian, 33
Sink, Robert, of Ashford, 16
Slyfield corn mill, Sy, 25

Smiles, Samuel, 38
Smith, Henrietta Jane, wife of Arthur Raby, 38
Smith, Hugh, of Stoke manor, Sy, 17, 19
Smithfield, London, 2, 3, 5, 41
South Wales, 1, 12, 34, 35–40
Southwark, 2, 20
Spain, 5
Spyers, James, jeweller, 31
Stanhope, Charles, 3rd Earl, iii
Stapleton, John, f, 13
Stanton, Derbs, iii
Steelyard, London, 12, 41
Stoke D'Abernon, Sy, 12, 16, 17–18, 22
Stoke House, 12; manor, 16, 17–18
Stour Partnership, 2; valley 1, 2
Stourbridge, Worcs, 1, 2
Stradey Estate, Llanelli, 35, 37, 38; furnace, 35
Sunderland, 1
Swalwell, Co Durham, 1
Swansea, 35

Sweden, 1, 2, 5

Tankerville, Lord, 19, 20n
Taylor, John, iron merchant, 12, 34
Taylor, John, pm, 23
Thames river, 9, 11; lock 30; Thames Lock mill, 20n
Thompson and Forman, of Coxes Lock mill, 34
Thursley furnace, Sy, 11
Tinmans Row, Cobham, 18, 19, 23, 24, 27
Trevithick, Richard, engineer, 37
Trummer, Christopher, f, 13
Tupper, John, miller, 26
Tyton, John, agent, 31

Vernon, Lord, 38
Victualling Board, 30
Vincent, Sir Francis, of Stoke Manor, 16, 17, 18, 19, 26

Walker, George, agent, 37

Warde, General George, 39
Warren furnace, Sx, 2, 3, 5, 6, 7, 15
Weald, 2–7, 11
Wedgwood, Josiah, 12, 15; Josiah II, 16; archives, 17, 20n
Welch, James, clerk, 31
Wells, Somerset, 39
West Indies, 38
Wey Navigation, 10, 11, 29, 30, 31; river 11; valley, 9
Weybridge, Sy, 9, 18, 31; mill 11, 12
Wheeler, Richard, iron mf, 2
Wheelwrights' Company, 2
White, Edward, of Ashford farm, 16
Whitmore & Binyon, engineers, of Wickham Market, Suffolk, 26
Wilkes, John 'Liberty', 16
Winlaton, Co Durham, 1
Wood, John, timber merchant, 20
Wood, Thomas W, silk throwster, 33, 34
Woodcock hammer, Sy, 3, 6
Wright & Prickett, Messrs, gun-fs, 7

Associated organisations

In the following list of organisations associated with the conference, contact addresses are those current in January 2000.

The Surrey Industrial History Group is a Group of the Surrey Archaeological Society. It aims to study, record and where appropriate preserve the remains of the former industries of the county. It holds meetings, lectures, visits and social events, undertakes recording and conservation projects and publishes a regular newsletter. Its publications include books on a variety of subjects and a series of *Guides* to the industrial history of the eleven administrative districts of the county.
Contact: The Membership Secretary, SIHG, c/o Surrey Archaeological Society, Castle Arch, Guildford, GU1 3SX
Website: http://shs.surreycc.gov.uk/sihg/

Addlestone Historical Society. The Society was founded in 1984 with the objective of bringing together those interested in the history and archaeology of Addlestone and its surrounding area. It holds regular monthly lecture meetings and arranges visits to places of interest. As well as a quarterly newsletter, the Society and its members publish material relating to the area. Its principal industrial archaeological feature is the mill complex at Coxes Lock on the Wey Navigation but it also has other sites of particular interest within its bounds.
Contact: The Secretary, Pam Brush, tel. 01932 872560

Esher District Local History Society. The Society was formed in May 1968 to encourage an interest in local history in the area comprising the former Esher Urban District. A variety of talks, walks and visits are arranged each month, including an annual coach outing. Members receive a regular Newsletter containing articles and items of local interest.
Contact: The Secretary, Mrs Christine Dall, 45 Telegraph Lane, Claygate KT10 0DT

Cyfeillion Amgueddfa Llanelli: Friends of Llanelli Museum. The Parc Howard Museum and Art Gallery holds collections of Llanelli pottery, exhibits of Welsh artists and items of local interest. The Friends aim to strengthen links with the community, publicise the Museum, help with research into the collections, encourage children and young people to attend, help with the acquisition of objects and further the development of Llanelli's heritage and history.
Contact: Hon Secretary, F R G Hughes, Glenvue, 27 Swiss Valley, Felinfoel, Llanelli SA15 8BS

Wealden Iron Research Group. The Wealden Iron Research Group (WIRG) was founded in 1968 to focus and initiate research into the extinct iron industry of the Sussex, Kent and Surrey Weald. It aims to promote the study of this subject, to collaborate with other groups, individuals and institutions with similar interests, and to publish research in *Wealden Iron*, its annual journal. *The Iron Industry of the Weald*, by Henry Cleere and David Crossley, first published in 1985, contains much of the Group's research. In 1981 the Group won the BBC's *Chronicle Award for Archaeology*. The Group's activities include two members' meetings a year, with visiting speakers and a summer visit. A field section organises a programme of fieldwalking, small-scale excavations and survey work between October and April, and experimental iron smelting is carried on by a team at a replica furnace on Ashdown Forest. A bi-annual newsletter contains a variety of news and matters of interest to members.
Contact: Hon. Secretary, 8 Woodview Crescent, Hildenborough, Tonbridge, Kent TN11 9HD
Website: www.np03.dial.pipex.com/wirg/

The Raby Family History Society carries out research into branches of the Raby family and maintains a database. It has co-ordinators in Australasia, Canada, Europe, South America and the USA. The Society issues a bi-annual newsletter and has published *The Boundary and Beyond: the Story of the Raby and Rabey Families*, edited by Graham Peter Rabey, 1995.
Contact: Bert Raby 5 Tower Place, Southampton SO30 3DL
e-mail addresses: bert@idea37.freeserve.co.uk ken@freewayuk.com